The
Last Black
Unicorn

The
Last Black
Unicorn

Tiffany Haddish

GALLERY BOOKS

New York   London   Toronto   Sydney   New Delhi

G

Gallery Books
An Imprint of Simon & Schuster, Inc.
1230 Avenue of the Americas
New York, NY 10020

First Gallery Books hardcover edition December 2017

GALLERY BOOKS and colophon are registered trademarks of Simon & Schuster, Inc.

For information about special discounts for bulk purchases, please contact Simon & Schuster
Special Sales at 1-866-506-1949 or business@simonandschuster.com.

The Simon & Schuster Speakers Bureau can bring authors to your live event.
For more information or to book an event, contact the Simon & Schuster Speakers
Bureau at 1-866-248-3049 or visit our website at www.simonspeakers.com.

Interior design by Jaime Putorti

Manufactured in the United States of America

10   9   8   7

Library of Congress Cataloging-in-Publication Data

Names: Haddish, Tiffany, 1979– author.
Title: The last black unicorn / Tiffany Haddish.
Description: New York : Gallery Books, [2017]
Identifiers: LCCN 2017038059 | ISBN 9781501181825 (hardback) | ISBN 9781501181832
    (trade paperback)
Subjects: LCSH: Haddish, Tiffany, 1979– | Haddish, Tiffany, 1979– Anecdotes. | African
    American women comedians—Biography. | African American actors—Biography. |
    BISAC: BIOGRAPHY & AUTOBIOGRAPHY / Rich & Famous.
Classification: LCC PN2287.H144 A3 2017 | DDC 792.7/6028092 [B] —dc23
    LC record available at https://lccn.loc.gov/2017038059

ISBN 978-1-5011-8182-5
ISBN 978-1-5011-8184-9 (ebook)

Contents

Invitation   vii

Mascots and Bar Mitzvahs: High School Years   1

Laugh Factory Comedy Camp   25

Family and Foster Care   37

Titus the Boyfriend   71

The Pimp Gets Pimped   99

Roscoe the Handicapped Angel   109

How I Got (Restarted) in Comedy   133

Dating   145

The Ex-Husband   161

The Long Road to Comedy Success   201

Tiffany's True Hollywood Stories   223

She Ready   253

Acknowledgments   277

Invitation

Hello, my name is Tiffany Haddish. I would like to invite you to read about a few of my experiences in life so far. I know that a lot of these stories will seem unbelievable. Shit, I look back over my life and I'm like, "For real, that happened?"

Either you will cry or laugh, and I try my best to figure out how to do the second one. I know life is no laughing matter, but having experiences can be. They can be the best learning lessons—just fuck ups but still lessons. That's how I think of my life, all my wins are lessons and all my failures are lessons that will one day become wins. I decided to write this book in the hope that someone will read it and feel like, "If she can do it, I know I can!"

I am inviting you to read it, because I never want you to say I didn't invite you to nothing. So come on in!

Mascots and Bar Mitzvahs: High School Years

School was hard for me, for lots of reasons. One was I couldn't read until, like, ninth grade. Also I was a foster kid for most of high school, and when my mom went nuts, I had to live with my grandma. That all sucked.

I got popular in high school, but before that, I wasn't so popular. Kids would tease me all the time in elementary and middle school. They'd say I got flies on me and I smell like onions.

The flies thing came from the moles on my face. I got one under my eye, I had one on my chin, and so on. That was kind of mean.

The onions thing was because my mom used to make eggs in the morning with onions in them. Every damn morning, I had to eat eggs and onions. That would just make you stink. The whole house would stink.

Yeah, it was mean to say I stunk like onions, but . . . I *did* stink like onions.

Kids used to make fun of me all the time about shit related to my mom. She didn't know how to do my hair. From kindergarten on up, I had the craziest hair.

I had long, pretty hair, but she didn't know how to do the ballies, or put it in a cute little ribbon. She only knew how to do the afro puffs, or just one big ponytail, but she didn't comb it all the way through, so I'd look like a cone head.

You know—black women, we got complicated hair. If you do it right, it's beautiful. But if you don't, it looks like some crow's nest.

In the black neighborhoods, little girls' hair is always cute. They've got the barrettes and all that. It's a big thing to have good hair as a black woman.

But not me. I had naps, and it was crazy. I would love when I would see my auntie Mary, because she would do my hair, and it would last for a few days. I'd try to sleep pretty. I'd put panties on my head, so I don't mess it up, and I'd sleep pretty.

But there was one nickname that stuck for a long time:

Dirty Ass Unicorn.

I had a wart growing on my forehead. I thought it was just an ugly mole. You couldn't help but notice. It was spiky and big, and I could not hide it. I used to try. I would wear bangs and stuff, nothing worked. It was growing out of my head. It was like a flower, and spiky, and it would curl into itself, like a horn.

The kids would make so much fun of me, they would talk about me so bad. It would make me so mad, it would hurt my feelings so much. I just wanted to hurt them back, but I didn't know how to hurt them back or what to say, because I actually did have this horn.

So all I could do was hurt myself. I would take scissors and I would try to cut off my horn, and then it would bleed. It would bleed down my face.

In school, in class, I would cut it off, and I would just sit there and wait for people to notice me. I would be bleeding down my face, and when they did notice, they'd freak out:

Kid 1: "Tiffany's bleeding!"

Kid 2: "Oh my God, oh my God, she cut her horn off, oh my God! Teacher!!"

They'd be trying to like take care of me, getting me paper towels and stuff. It made them care about me. Hurting myself made them stop hurting me and care about me.

Teacher: "Tiffany, why'd you do that?"

Tiffany: "Because they keep talking bad about my horn. I want to cut it off, so they can't talk about it no more."

The teachers never had no response to that.

Then I'd be walking around for three or four days with a hole in my forehead, 'cause I done cut it off. Then it would just grow right back. Like, in five days, it would be right back.

Finally, one day I was crying about this to my grandma. She grabbed me and started looking at my head:

Grandma: "Child, that ain't no damn mole. That a wart."

Tiffany: "What's a wart?"

Grandma: "It's nasty is what it is. You got HPV. What'chu been touching on, child?"

Tiffany: "What's HPV?"

Grandma: "It's a nasty wart that nasty people get after they do nasty things."

That was messed up by my grandma. Now that I'm older, I learned that skin warts is nothing like genital warts. They're totally different. But in my grandma's eyes, I was nasty. I was doing something nasty.

The good news is that she got it burnt off. She took me to the doctor to confirm it was a wart and then burnt that shit right off.

That's how the Dirty Ass Unicorn died and the Last Black Unicorn was born.

High school was way better for me.

I went to a school called El Camino Real. It was 3 percent black. It was mostly white and Hispanic and Asian—and pretty much all of them were rich.

I got bused from South Central LA. I woke up every morning about 5 a.m. to catch the bus at 6:15. I had to walk to the bus stop in the cold every morning. I mean, this is LA, so it's not like there was snow. But for me, sixty degrees is freezing.

What was funny about high school was that all the things that got made fun of in elementary school, they were valued in high school. I was a great talker and had a unique style—"poor as fuck chic"—these were good qualities in a rich suburban school, where everyone else was the same. I stood out.

But the truth is, the main reason I ended up being successful in high school was because of everything I did while trying to get with this one dude, Audie.

I was stalking him. I would send him candygrams. Remember candygrams? I sent him A LOT of candygrams. I gave him a Snickers every week, till we was in twelfth grade. That dude probably has a mouth full of cavities because of me. I would try to write him notes, but I was illiterate, so everything was wrong. It was the worst:

"Audie, yo how bout we date er som fing?"

I was in ninth grade, and straight up I could not read or write.

I could only read three-letter words or things you see on TV. It was like first- or second-grade reading level.

You wanna hear some real crazy shit? I was in AP classes (where you can get college credit in high school), while not being able to read!

I could not spell or read, but I knew how to talk. I would game people. I would game everybody. It's easy to game school, once you realize that the rules are bullshit and you can get around them.

For example, whenever I had to read something, I would get someone else to read it to me. There was this one dude who was really smart, and he had a deep voice. I would be like, "Oh my God, Curtis, could you read this to me, I love hearing your voice." I had the greatest memory, so if he read to me I would memorize it instantly, and then if we had to read out loud in class, I would just say what he had said.

The problem would be when I would "read" the wrong paragraph. The teacher would say:

Teacher: "What are you talking about, Tiffany? You read the last paragraph. I want you to read the first one."

Tiffany: "I got to pee, I'm sorry."

I'd get up and run out the classroom. I had a lot of those types of emergencies my ninth-grade year.

Multiple choice tests were easy to fake. I would make people laugh, make 'em want to be my friend, and then, they would let me copy off of them. Essay tests were harder to fake, but I found a way. Here's what I did:

I would just tell the teacher I was sick, or find a way to take the test later. Then I'd ask a friend, "What'd you say on your essay? Tell me everything." They would tell me, I would memorize their words, and I'd just repeat them. My essay would be full of misspellings and grammar mistakes, but it would pretty much have whatever somebody else's essay had.

Now, it seems crazy that I could not read or write. My memory was really good, so it didn't make no sense. I just couldn't read. You know what it was? I just didn't believe I could. I thought I was stupid.

Before high school, I was told I was stupid every day. My stepdad used to tell me I was stupid all the time. My mama said it every day. My grandma sometimes. Definitely other kids at school. I believed I was stupid, so I guess I just didn't think I could do it. I never tried.

I used to hate when people called me stupid. That would make me so angry. I would want to fight you for calling me stupid. But you know what's so funny? As an adult, when I was working at the airline, one of my coworkers called me stupid. I said:

Tiffany: "You call me stupid one more damn time, we're gonna have a straight-up fight in here."

Coworker: "You do realize I'm trying to tell you that you're funny. I think you're funny. That's why I'm saying that. Like, you stupid funny."

Tiffany: "Oh, shit. My bad. I won't fight you over no compliment."

I started thinking, maybe all these years people been trying to tell me I was funny. Here I'm thinking they were trying to say I'm dumb, 'cause I felt dumb.

But back to being illiterate and trying to date Audie:

Audie ended up outing my lack of reading and writing, but not on purpose. Audie was in drama class, so I got into drama class. My thinking was that Audie was the only black dude in drama, and if I joined, I would be the only black girl in drama. I thought to myself, *I bet we going to be kissing. We're going to have to be husband and wife or something. They're going to have to put us together. This school racist. They're going to have to put us together.*

But no. These motherfuckers had to be all liberal and integrated and shit. Audie got to have a Hispanic wife in the play. But I'm going to have to be a single mom?

Tiffany: "Why do I still got to be a statistic? This is not fair. I want to kiss Audie."

Teacher: "What?"

And the shitty part was that Audie was cool with it. Man, I sent him so many Snickers, and he never gave me any sugar.

It was the drama teacher who figured out I couldn't read. It was the end of my ninth-grade year. She asked me to stay after class, and by this time, she knew my hustle. She trapped me.

Miss Gree: "Tiffany, I want you to try this part. It's a role opposite Audie."

Tiffany: "Yeah, girl, I'm in!"

Miss Gree: "Great, I thought you might like it. Here, read this page, let's see how you do."

Tiffany: "Okay, Miss Gree, lemme take the script home and work on it, and I'll do it for you tomorrow."

Miss Gree: "I love your work ethic, Tiffany. But no. I'm going to need you to read this right now."

Tiffany: "Uh . . . I'm not feeling well though, for real."

Miss Gree: "You seemed very healthy thirty seconds ago. This must be a rapid virus."

Tiffany: "Oh yeah, it could be Ebola. I better get to the nurse before I infect you."

Miss Gree: "Tiffany . . . can you read?"

Tiffany: "I can read!"

Miss Gree: "Then just read this paragraph before you go see the nurse. Read this and you have the part."

Tiffany: "You so pretty, Miss Gree. Did you change your hair?"

She was like no, no, no, no, no. She caught me.

But she was so cool about it. She didn't tell anyone. She got me out of nutrition class, and had me come in every day and learn to read with her. She took me from first-grade level to ninth-grade level in like, a month. She just sat with me and showed me, and it was no problem.

Once I could read, man, it was like I had a superpower! I wasn't stupid! All them words made sense!

She had me get into competitive monologue. I had already been in a drama festival as part of a team, and my team won first place for *Macbeth*, but I was just a witch. Easy shit, like, "Double double toil and trouble." Super easy.

Now she had me do the Shakespeare Festival. It was a monologue, so I played all the characters. I was doing pretty well at some of the smaller competitions, but then there was the big one.

And I won first place. I beat out 375 drama kids.

When they called me as the winner, it was just me standing there onstage along with this one white guy. We were the finalists. He had won every year previously, so everyone expected him to win again. When they called my name, I kinda freaked out. I remember just being like, "Whooaaa." I was just trembling all over, and then I started doing the Running Man right onstage. The lady who was presenting the award got mad:

Presenter: "Act like a lady. Act like a lady!"

Tiffany: "I am! I am!"

I think that's the very first time I had an orgasm. I'm pretty sure I had one onstage. Then, I didn't know what it was. I just started trembling and freaking out and getting sweats and tingling. Man, I was so happy.

You know what I was most happy about?

This would mean I was going to be able to buy my first pair of shoes on my own.

You see, I had made a bet. A week before the big competition, my aunt's boyfriend was down on me:

Boyfriend: "You're not gonna do it. That drama shit is a white thing. You're not going to make it."

Tiffany: "I've won before, at smaller meets. I did good."

Boyfriend: "They ain't gonna pick you. This Shakespeare. This a white thing."

Tiffany: "I bet you I'm gonna win!"

Boyfriend: "Child, please. I bet you $100 you ain't gonna win."

When I got home, I ran in with my trophy:

Auntie: "You won?"

Tiffany: "I sure did. Got my trophy and everything!"

Boyfriend: "You didn't win! You robbed some white kid for his trophy!"

Best believe I got my $100 out of him. And I used that $100 to buy a pair of Doc Martens boots.

Everybody had them, and most importantly, Audie said he liked girls that wore Doc Martens boots. He didn't think I could ever afford a pair. Until then, I had been wearing Payless shoes that looked kind of like the boots, but they were regular shoes. I'd wear black socks all the way up to my knees, so it'd look like I had it going on. But I didn't. I didn't have it going on.

But I won. I beat 375 drama kids for a pair of Doc Martens boots.

The next day, I missed the school bus and went all the way to the Shoe Warehouse and bought my Doc Martens boots, and then I caught the MTA to school. I showed up at the school about three or four hours late and I was like, bam! Stomping through school in my Doc Martens boots.

And then Audie still didn't like me. He still didn't want me.

So I became the school mascot. My tenth-grade year, I became the Conquistador, the Spanish soldier mascot of El Camino Real High School.

At first, I tried to join the cheerleading squad, but the cheerleaders had too many rules. Their rules were nonsense. Like you can't cuss, you got to be on time, you have to wear mascara every day, you have to have your hair done pretty every day. All these rules. And you can't just dance when you feel like it. I was like:

Tiffany: "What kind of rules you got for the mascot?"

Teacher: "The mascot doesn't have any rules."

Tiffany: "That's what I want to be, then—the mascot."

Nobody had tried out to be the mascot, except me. So I got it.

The first time I mascoted, I didn't have the uniform yet. It was too big for me, so I had my grandma do alterations on it. I had a T-shirt, and I wrote on it in big black letters:

"Will have uniform in 2 weeks. Grandma doin' it."

People loved it.

My routine was dope. I would be running up and down the field with my megaphone, telling people what to do, leading cheers.

Tiffany: "El Cam, what?"

Crowd: "Mino!"

Tiffany: "El Cam, whaaaaat?"

Crowd: "MINO!"

Tiffany: "You know!"

Crowd: "WE KNOW!"

I would pass out candy, I would bring people down from the stands and do dance-offs, I would do all kinds of fun stuff like that. I would be watching ESPN to see what the professional mascots do, and then I'd be ripping off their techniques. I was pretty awesome at this.

The only reason I even wanted to be on the cheerleading squad (or, later, a mascot) was so I could be with the football players, because Audie also played football. But also, there was some other fine guys that played football, so I figured this would be a great way to get a boyfriend and get laid.

None of that worked out, but I did become the most popular girl in school. They even put a plaque on the wall with my name on it. It's still on the wall. And best of all—by my senior year, I was getting PAID to be the high school mascot.

I was paid $50 a game. That was unprecedented for my high school.

See, that happened because Audie told me he couldn't be with me. It was during my eleventh-grade year.

Audie: "I can't date no mascot. I'm not going to have no mascot girlfriend. They going to be calling me the mascot assistant. I don't think so."

To make Audie jealous, I had gotten another boyfriend on the football team. He was a grade under me, and he used to carry my bag for me. So they started calling him the assistant mascot.

Audie: "See man, that's why I don't fuck with Tiffany. I ain't no assistant mascot."

My senior year, my boyfriend broke up with me, because he got tired of his friends calling him the assistant mascot. He didn't want to get clowned like that. I told the principal I had to quit. I told everybody I quit, because I'm looking for a boyfriend. They thought it was a joke, but then when they saw I wasn't at the first game my senior year, they was like, "We ain't going to the next game."

The attendance numbers went way down. Like, half the people didn't show up to the second game, because the Conquistador had retired. The Dean called me in:

Dean: "What's it going to take to get you back on the field, Haddish?"

Tiffany: "A boyfriend."

Dean: "I can't get you a boyfriend. What else can we do?"

Tiffany: "A boyfriend is what I need."

Dean: "How about we give you double credits?"

Tiffany: "I got credits. I go to summer school every year. I got credits. I need a boyfriend."

Dean: "Tiffany, please, be reasonable. I can't get you a boyfriend. How about we compensate you the candy sales?"

Tiffany: "No. I want a boyfriend."

Dean: "What else, Tiffany? What else?"

Tiffany: "Fine . . . gimme $100 per game."

Dean: "No, we can't give you $100. How about $25?"

Tiffany: "$75."

Dean: "I can't do $75. I can't very well compensate you $75 from candy."

Tiffany: "No, this ain't about candy. This is my time for not having no boyfriend. I'm going to need to get my hair done. I need to get my nails done. I'm going to have to start being a fly chick if I want a boyfriend, and being a mascot is not going to help me get no boyfriend, so I can't do it."

Dean: "$50, Haddish, and that's the most I can do, and you're going to have to bring the candy receipts."

Tiffany: "You got it. You got it, Mr. Dean."

Boom! I was getting paid $50 a game my senior year. I had my hair and nails done, too.

Being paid to be a mascot was cool and all, but what was really cool was that it got me my first real paying entertainment job.

I became an "energy producer" at Bar Mitzvahs. Energy pro-

ducer is what white suburban people call a "hype man." I was basically the Flava Flav of Bar Mitzvahs.

I used to get that party cracking. And eventually, I got into MC-
ing and DJing. I did it for eleven years. I did over five hundred Bar
Mitzvahs.

It started when I was at a school dance. I was tearing it up.
There was a big circle around me, 'cause I was dancing and having
fun with people and all that. Whenever I party, man, there's always
a circle. They was like, "Go Tiffany! Go Tiffany!"

The school dance had a professional DJ. He came up to me
afterwards:

DJ: "Tiff, you're amazing. Do you ever do parties?"

Tiffany: "I love to party."

DJ: "I'd love for you to work for my company. We do execu-
tive parties and Bar Mitzvahs. Here is my card, give me a
call, let's set up a meeting."

I'm thinking this dude is disgusting. The problem was, I didn't
know what a Bar Mitzvah was. I had no clue. It just sounded nasty.
I thought he was so nasty, but I didn't want to be rude to him, so I
took his card. I took it back to my grandma.

Tiffany: "Grandma, this man asked me to *dance* at execu-
tive parties and Bar Mitzvahs. Can you believe this?"

Grandma: "Girl, you better call him. That's getting close to
your people."

Tiffany: "What do you mean 'getting close to my people.'"

Grandma: "Girl, you Jewish."

Tiffany: "No, I'm not. I'm a Jehovah Witness."

Grandma: "No, you not a Jehovah Witness. You're Jewish. Jehovah's Witness is a religion. Your people is Jewish."

She was talking about my father. He is actually Jewish. My father's from Eritrea, which is right next to Ethiopia. There are actually a lot of Jews in the Horn of Africa, and even though he was black, he was still Jewish.

Tiffany: "My people?"

Grandma: "You're Jewish. Your people. You know, you need to know about your other side of the family. Your daddy's side." .

Tiffany: "Well, why don't I even know my daddy?"

Grandma: " 'Cause he made some mistakes and he had to get on. He sent money though. All them dance classes I got you when you was a little girl and gymnastics classes you took when you was a little girl. That was from your dad. He would send me money and I would put you in the classes."

Man, no one ever told me that. That was crazy to me, that my daddy had been sending money and stuff.

Grandma: "We calling that man."

Tiffany: "I don't want to call that man. He want me to get on the bar and show my mitzvah."

Grandma: "What are you talking about child?"

Tiffany: "You know, showing my mitzvah! I don't want to be no stripper, Grandma!"

Grandma: "Oh Lord, child please."

I had thought "Bar Mitzvah" meant you get on the bar and show your mitzvah—you know, like your cootchie. Because the way he was talking to me, I was creeped out, and that's what I thought he meant.

She called that man and she drove me all the way to this man's office, at his house. It wasn't no damn office. He was only eighteen. He's just running this little DJ company out of his mama's house. He set his room up, and the name of his company was Enterprise Entertainment, because he was into *Star Trek*. He had painted the whole room black, and it had glow-in-the-dark stars all over it. He had a futon that he called his couch and a little desk.

His name was Tim. We called him DJ Timbo. Me and my grandma were sitting there on his futon as he explained the ins and outs of Bar Mitzvahs. He had started with his uncle (DJ'ing at a company called Hart to Hart) when he was twelve, and then he split off and started his own company.

He wanted me to be his first employee at his company. He thought we could do well.

Grandma: "You think that a little black girl is going to do okay at a Bar Mitzvah, baby? You think that she can work at a Bar Mitzvah?"

DJ Timbo: "I definitely think so. She has the energy. She has a great smile. Great personality. I think she can do it."

Grandma: "You want it, baby?"

Tiffany: "Yeah."

Grandma: "How much you going to pay my baby?"

DJ Timbo: "I'm going to give her $40 a party."

Grandma: "You want to make $40 a party?"

Tiffany: "Sounds good to me."

Then he started booking me for parties. I'll never forget the very first party I did. I got to work it with the brother of DJ Timbo, Thomas Ian Nicholas. He was in the movie *Rookie of the Year*. He was working the party too, so I was like, "Oh my."

He was dancing with me, and he was like, "This is how you got to do it."

I was like, "Boy, this kid is sure trying to be helpful to me. He must think I'm hot."

At the end of the party, I asked him for his number. He told me I was a weirdo, and he didn't give it to me. I had been too aggressive.

Anyway, afterwards, DJ Timbo wrote me a letter and mailed it to me. Like, physical mail. It said I was horrible. He said that I needed to not be following one kid around the whole time, especially one that's also working the party. I had to be more dedicated, more focused. You have to keep your eyes on the whole party, and all that stuff. It was a serious rundown of everything I did wrong. He wrote:

"And here's your $40. If you think you can do it, give me a call back, and if you don't think you can handle it, don't call me."

As soon as I read that, I called him:

Tiffany: "Man, I can do all of this and then some. Boy please, when is the next party?"

The next party, I was pumped up. Dancing with everybody. Dancing with the old people. Dancing with the young people. Getting all the people to follow me. Doing all my routines and stuff. I was doing stuff that I did on the football field for the games. At the Bar Mitzvahs, I was doing waves and all kind of stuff. I killed it. And that was my weekend work for like, ten years after that.

After two years, I ended up becoming one of the MCs. I started making like $200 a party, $300 a party on the weekends. For a teenager, that's dope.

The only downside to the Bar Mitzvahs was that I killed a man once.

I'm not even kidding.

At this point, I was about twenty. I had been doing Bar Mitzvahs for four years, and I was good by then. I would do a Bar Mitzvah right.

This one was up in the Valley. I was dancing, getting the crowd hyped, and I saw an old man over there, just looking mopey. It's my job to get everyone hyped, so I danced over to him.

Tiffany: "Come on, you want to dance with me?"

Old Man: "No, no, no."

Tiffany: "Come on, you know you want to dance. You know you want to!"

Old Man: "No, no, I'm old, dance with the young people."

He was saying no, but I could tell he meant yes, so I grabbed his hand, and he got up with me, and he came to the dance floor. And then I grabbed him by his tie and went all in.

Tiffany: "Yeaaaaaaaah boy, get it done!"

Old Man: "Whooooo!"

And he was into it and enjoying it, and people were cheering, and the party started to jump off.

I let go of his tie, and we started dancing a little simple two-step. And then I turned around on him and gave him a little booty pop, right? Just a little one, right in his old man crotch, like pop-pop. I sprang back up and kept dancing, and then I saw people were staring at me, shocked.

I turned back around, and he was on the ground. On his back, holding his chest.

Tiffany: "Oh shit. Oh shit!"

Everybody was rushing over. There were some doctors in attendance who were working on him, and they called an ambulance. They were doing CPR on him and all of that.

But it was the weirdest thing: he was smiling the whole time. I swear to God that man was smiling.

The ambulance came, and they took him to the hospital. And with the ambulance came the police. So, I just knew I was going to jail. I just figured that since I'm the only black person at this party, the police are there for me. They're going to say I killed this man. I was fixing to go to jail, that was it. I was trying to figure out who to call, and mentally preparing myself for going to jail.

Police: "Okay, I think that wraps it. If we have any other questions, we'll let you know."

And they just left. What's going on?

That man ended up dying in the hospital. I was home, I'm thinking the police were going to show up to my house any day now to take me to jail.

And I decided I quit. No more dancing, no more Bar Mitzvahs, nothing. I was done. I stopped doing them. DJ Timbo was calling me and calling me, telling me people were requesting me.

Tiffany: "I can't do it, I can't. I just can't right now. This is not a good time. I don't feel safe."

DJ Timbo: "Tiffany, they are asking for you specifically. They want you there."

Tiffany: "I don't feel like people should be around me. I'm not safe."

DJ Timbo: "Tiffany, your ass is not deadly."

Tiffany: "No, my ass *is* deadly. That man is dead."

DJ Timbo: "Tiffany, that man was old. It was his time. He was probably happy. It was probably the first time he ever danced with a black girl in his life. It was the happiest moment of his life."

But Timbo couldn't talk me into doing them. That man hadn't wanted to dance at first, and I made him, and then I booty popped him . . . and now he's dead! I just felt like a booty assassin.

Then, I got a letter from his daughter. She tipped me—she sent me a big tip and told me thank you. She said they'd never seen him that happy, they hadn't seen him smile like that or that happy in a long time. And she said that they knew this was coming, he was in his late eighties, and they had been waiting for him to pass. And they appreciated everything that I did, and I should not blame myself.

She made some good points. And you know, she did tell me to dance with everybody. She specifically said to get all the older people up. So maybe she wanted me to kill him? I don't know.

After that letter, I went back to doing Bar Mitzvahs. At that point, they were paying me $400 a party. The money was too good.

Laugh Factory
Comedy Camp

I started doing comedy at fifteen. I was getting in trouble in school, that's what got me into it. It was all because of this one teacher.

I was talking too much in class, and my teacher was always sending me to the principal's office. The social worker was getting tired of coming up to the school, and the principal was tired of calling the social worker.

Come to think of it, it wasn't just talking. This teacher kept saying I was racist, but I didn't think I was being racist. I thought I was being funny.

My whole thing was just to make everybody laugh. If I could do that, then they'd let me copy their homework and they'd help me on tests.

One of the ways I made everyone laugh was to make up these imaginary friends. I had a female imaginary friend that I called Carmelita and a little bird that I called Cracker. I would talk to them in the hallways and during class, and if somebody sat down next to me, I'd be like:

Tiffany: "Wait, watch out. You're sitting on Carmelita's lap. She likes that, though. Wiggle on her."

And they would jump up and be like, "What are you talking about?" And then, eventually, they would become my friends. People would be like, "You crazy. You silly. I like you." It worked really well for me. It's basically how I made it through school.

Every time we would take a test, I would turn my head toward my shoulder, and I would be like, "Cracker want a Polly?" I had some crackers, and I would crumble them up on my shoulder for my imaginary bird, and people would be laughing. Then they'd let me cheat off of them.

The teacher didn't know I was cheating though, that's not why she was always sending me to the principal's office. During one test, I said:

Tiffany: "What's the answer to number seven, Cracker?"

You know, because that was my imaginary bird's name. But my teacher thought I was being racist against her.

Teacher: "You go straight to the principal's office. You can't be racist in here."

This happened a few times, and everybody would laugh. I would just tell the principal the same thing each time.

Tiffany: "I was talking to my friend, my imaginary bird."

Principal: "Oh, God, again with the imaginary friends?"

After like the fifth time, my social worker couldn't take it anymore.

Social Worker: "Tiffany, you got two choices this summer coming up. You can go to the Laugh Factory Comedy Camp, or you can go to psychiatric therapy. Which one do you want to do, 'cause something is wrong with you."

Tiffany: "Which one got drugs?"

Social Worker: "Therapy."

I didn't want no drugs, I had seen how those fuck people up. So I went to the comedy camp.

Laugh Factory Comedy Camp was kinda perfect, except how long it took to get there. I'd have to catch the bus up there from 54th and Western, and I would ride all the way up to the Laugh Factory camp. Riding that bus, you would see the demographics of the people change, as you went from South Central through Hollywood. I remember getting on the bus feeling poor. But as we would get to Hollywood, I would see a little bit higher class of people boarding the bus. I felt like I was literally moving up in the world.

I would go up there every week, and I got to meet a lot of different comedians. A lot of mentors would come in. Dane Cook showed up. Chris Spencer. All the Wayans brothers came one day. Harland Williams came by, and Quincy Jones.

I remember the day Quincy Jones came in there, I was like:

Tiffany: "What is he doing here? He ain't funny."

But he was saying how comedy is like music, and it's about the rhythm of the words. Like if you really listen to a joke, it has a melody to the punchline. I got that, it really helped me.

Charles Fleischer was there. I was so excited about Charles Fleischer, 'cause he does the voice of Roger Rabbit. The character I've been emulating the most, just trying to be funny—and now, the guy who does this character's voice is teaching me, talking to me.

I liked Charles Fleischer a lot, but he was all intent on telling me not to do bathroom humor, which I did not agree with. He was like:

Charles: "You're a pretty girl. You shouldn't do bathroom humor."

I had a joke about going to a public bathroom, and then an old lady comes in the stall next to you, and she be making weird noises, and I imitated the lady's noises and stuff. He said I shouldn't do bathroom humor.

When he said I was too pretty to do bathroom humor, at first I was flattered. That was the first time a man told me I was pretty. Come to think of it later, that might have been a little creepy. But I think he was just trying to be nice, so it's cool.

Being in that comedy camp was the first time I felt safe. I didn't think anything bad was gonna happen. That was maybe my favorite part about Laugh Factory Comedy Camp.

By that point, I had lived in a few foster places and knew a few things. If a grown man tells you that you pretty, he's gonna be trying to touch on you soon, and all kinds of terrible stuff is gonna happen.

But at comedy camp, that man told me I'm pretty, but I didn't feel like it was dangerous. He cared about me and was saying a nice thing. He was trying to help me.

My biggest influence was probably Richard Pryor. He came in there, and I'm telling my jokes, and he stopped me in the middle of telling my jokes:

Richard: "Stop, stop, stop. What are you doing?"

Tiffany: "I'm telling a joke."

Richard: "No, you're not."

Tiffany: "Yes, I am."

Richard: "No, you're not."

Tiffany: "YES, I AM!"

Richard: "NO, YOU ARE NOT!"

Me and Richard Pryor. Squabbling back and forth right on-stage.

Tiffany: "Well, what'chu you think I'm doing up here?"

Richard: "You're getting on my goddam nerves, that's what'chu doing! Look, people don't come to comedy shows because they want to hear about your problems, or about politics, or what's going on in the world, or celebrities. They don't care. They come to comedy shows to have fun. So when you're onstage, you need to be having fun. If you're having fun, they're having fun. If you not having fun, they looking at you like 'what the hell did I spend my money on?' *So you need to have fun."*

Richard Pryor gave me that advice, at the Laugh Factory Comedy Camp, when I was fifteen.

I'd had a pretty rough life to that point, and I'd had some bad shit come my way, but I was pretty lucky for that experience. I try to take that philosophy and apply it to everything I do in life. That's why I think my life turned out as good as it has. Because all the time, I'm just trying to have fun.

Wherever you are, thank you, Richard. That meant so much to me, and to this day I try to have fun every time I'm onstage, because of you.

When I was in Laugh Factory Comedy Camp, the Channel Two news came, and they did a story on me. But since I was a foster kid, I had to go to the courthouse to get permission to be on television. Since foster kids are technically state property, I couldn't be on TV without the court's permission. It's just like you would have to have your parents' permission to be on television, I had to have the court's permission. That was my parents at the time—the state of California.

My social worker didn't want to go down to the courts to help me. It was summertime, so I was out of school. I decided I was gonna go down to the courthouse and get this permission myself.

I caught the bus and took about three transfers to get all the way to the family courts, which is, like, in the city of Alhambra or some shit.

I went to the clerk, I found out who my judge was, I went into his courtroom. He wasn't noticing me, not paying me any attention, the bailiff wouldn't talk to me. I was like, *Wow, just like my real parents, my state parents don't care either.* Then, I finally stood up, and I asked the bailiff:

Tiffany: "Can I talk to the judge?"

Bailiff: "What you got?"

He took the papers to the judge, and he came back.

Bailiff: "It's not one of the cases on file, so we can't do it."

I went back down to the clerk's office.

Tiffany: "Can you make it so I can see the judge?"

Clerk: "We'll send your case up to the courtroom. But you have to come back tomorrow."

I went through all that *again* the next day, and they were still not paying attention to me.

But this time, I was prepared. I had brought a Walkman, a magazine, chewing gum, a soda—all the stuff they say not to have. Today, I was going to get their attention. They were not gonna ignore me.

So I was flipping the magazine, popping the bubblegum, and drinking a soda, and the judge was trying not to notice. Then all of a sudden, he kind of snaps:

Judge: "Who are you? What are you doing in my courthouse?"

Tiffany: "I'm Tiffany Haddish. I'm here so you can sign my papers."

Judge: "What are these papers for?"

Tiffany: "I'm trying to be on the news. I need to be on the news."

Judge: "What do you need to be on the news for?"

Tiffany: "I'm at the Laugh Factory Comedy Camp, I'm gonna be a world-famous comedian, and I need you to sign this paperwork, so that I can be on the news story they want to do about me."

Judge: "And why do you need to be on the news to be a world-famous comedian?"

Tiffany: "Because, then that way, my dad's gonna see me, he gonna be really proud, then everybody gonna be really proud. I'm gonna be really funny, I'm gonna make people laugh, and that's gonna be my job forever, and I'mma be a world-famous comedian, and then I'll be happy."

He looked at me over his glasses, staring at me for a second. Everyone in the courthouse was dead quiet.

Judge: "Are you sure about all of this?"

Tiffany: "Yes, I am very sure. I know this."

Judge: "Well, if you act onstage as funny as you act now, then you probably will be a world-famous comedian."

Then he read my case. He asked me:

Judge: "Do you know who your father is?"

Tiffany: "Nope. I haven't seen him since I was three."

Judge: "Where's your mom?"

Tiffany: "She's locked down in a mental facility. She crazy."

Then he signed the paper.
I was all happy. That bus ride back felt much shorter.

The news came, and they filmed me. It went real good, and they told me when it would be on, and I was real excited.

Then the day it was supposed to come on, that day, Princess Diana goes and gets killed in a car wreck.

I got bumped. It's cool, though. I wasn't mad. She was a princess, I get it.

It was two months before it finally came on the air. I was so happy watching it. I felt like a star already. It was the first time I had ever seen myself as valuable, worth people's time or attention.

After that comedy camp, they started letting me do stand-up. Like, onstage. Sometimes, I would get to MC, sometimes do a set. At first, it was all during the day.

Later, I was going up to the Laugh Factory on a Friday or Saturday night. Night shows are much bigger. I was too young to go real late, but they would let me go up on the eight o'clock show and get like five minutes. I would do my set, and I would leave. I wasn't allowed to stay in there, 'cause of the alcohol.

And they would give me like ten or fifteen bucks. That was just enough to cover bus fare, but it was cool. I was getting paid to tell jokes. I was on my way.

I did that all through high school, till I was like eighteen. And then, I had to quit.

I had to quit comedy, because I was homeless, and I was supposed to go to NYU, and I had no idea what to do.

I know, it's confusing. Here's how it went:

Once I turned eighteen, my grandma sat me down.

Grandma: "Since I ain't getting paid for you now, you need to go to school. You grown. Go on, get out there. You got friends. You'll make it."

I had gotten accepted into NYU, but they weren't paying my way. I didn't have no money, and my grandma was still taking care of my brothers and sisters. I was like, *What if something happens to her? Who's gonna be here for them?*

So I decided I'm gonna go to Santa Monica Community College, and I'm gonna get a job.

I was basically couch surfing then. I was just going to all my friends' houses. Homeless as hell, just traveling around with my plastic bins. The ones with wheels on them and stuff.

At that point, I had to stop doing comedy. I was only making

$10 or $15 a show. I couldn't live off of that. I was emancipated, and I needed a roof over my head. Getting paid $10 or $15 wasn't gonna cut it. I could not find time to go to college, and work, and then also take a bus to do comedy. It just didn't work.

I was eighteen. To survive, I had to quit comedy.

Family and Foster Care

The Car Wreck

Where do I even start with my family?

I should probably start with the car accident. That's when everything changed.

Before the car accident, my mom had it together. She had two small businesses going, she was a manager at a U.S. post office, and she owned two houses on the same street.

At that point, she was married to my stepfather. I'll call him Step-Father. He sucked. He was always cheating on her, but it didn't matter to her. She worshiped the ground he walked on. Whatever mistakes he made, she didn't care. He knocked up one of the employees of her businesses. She argued with him, but she didn't leave him. She just loved that man. He could never do wrong, even when he did a lot of wrong.

She had three kids by him, all younger than me. I was the oldest. I felt like she loved them way more because she loved their dad. She didn't love my dad. He left when I was real young.

I was around seven when Step-Father knocked up my mom's employee, so he and my mom moved us all out to Pomona, and then to Colton. She was still trying to work in Marina del Rey after she had my sister. It was like she was working the graveyard shift. She had to drop us off at my grandmother's every day. This one day when I was eight I told her she didn't have to do it.

Tiffany: "Mom, let me babysit. I know how to make bottles. I know how to change diapers. We're going to go to bed in about two hours. I know how to make hot dogs, rice. I know how to cook everything. We're about to go to bed, and when you get home we'll be waking up."

Mom: "I'm running late. Okay."

She never came back.

Two days went by. She did not come home. Step-Father didn't come home, either. No one came home. Step-Father used to come home every night, but he didn't come home at all.

I called my grandma, and my grandma said she hadn't heard from my mom. By the third day, my grandma came out to where we were. She called Step-Father's auntie and his auntie said:

Auntie: "Oh, she's in the hospital in Pomona. She had a car accident on the 10 Freeway. You didn't know?"

Grandma: "Why didn't nobody tell me? How do you know and I don't know?"

Auntie: "Well, Step-Father knew."

Step-Father knew, and he didn't do nothing.

They wouldn't let me see my mom for two months. The accident was real bad. Her head was open and all this stuff. They didn't tell me the details, they just looked at me and told me my mama would be fine. I would always think, *If she's gonna be fine, why can't I see her?*

When we finally got to see her, I was not prepared. She looked like a monster. Her eyes were black, and she had bandages across her head. She was swollen. Her whole body was swollen.

She didn't look like my mama.

She had to learn to walk again. And talk, and eat, and everything. She did not remember any of my brothers and sisters. She just remembered me, and she was saying things like:

Mom: "You look just like my daughter, Tiffany. You should meet my daughter. She's only three."

Tiffany: "I am Tiffany. I am your daughter."

It kind of made me feel really good, because I didn't necessarily like my brothers and sisters that much. I felt like she loved them way more than she loved me.

When she was in the hospital for three months, learning how to do all that stuff again, me and my siblings were with our grandmother.

When she got out of the hospital, me and my siblings went back to live with her. Everything was totally different after that.

I had to grow up fast. I taught her how to tie her shoe, like she had taught me how to tie my shoe. I taught her how to put her pants on, like she had taught me to put pants on. I was showing her how to make hot dogs like she showed me how to make hot dogs. Everything she had taught me, I was teaching her back.

That was bad enough, but after that accident, oh my God, she would say the worst things to me. I felt like all of the inner thoughts that she used to have before the accident, but she never said out loud, would all come out. She'd be like:

Mom: "Oh, you look like your ugly-ass daddy. Oh, God, where's my husband at? I'm so sick of looking at your ugly ass."

I guess that is common for people with a brain injury. They talk crazy, and all kinds of mean stuff comes out.

It was pretty clear that my mama did not like me. She did not. She loved me but she did not like me. I think it was because I reminded her of my father.

Mom: "You look like your father's ugly ass. I hate him."

All like that, all the time, until I was twelve. Constantly telling me I'm ugly, I'm stupid, I'm not worth nothing. I just felt stupid and not important, but I loved this woman so much. I'd just do whatever, 'cause I loved her. She was the first person I'd ever loved.

And now, after this car wreck, she hated me. She even said that to me at times.

Tiffany: "Mom, how are you feeling?"

Mom: "I hate you."

It took her maybe two months to really get acclimated with my brothers and sisters, so during that time I was nurturing them. I was nurturing everybody.

And because of this, I was doing really bad in school.

My grandma, though, she would come and help. And my great-granny would come, and they would help. My grandma would always be like:

Grandma: "I'm proud of you. Look at all you did, you're a good daughter."

She could see what I was doing for the family. She and my great-granny saw it. My mom would cuss me out in front of them:

Mom: "Get that ugly-ass girl out of here. Why you don't comb your hair? Ugh, you're so ugly."

Tiffany: "I'll try. I'll try to comb my hair."

Grandma: "Come here, I'll comb your hair. You are not ugly. Your mom is just tired. She's bad when she's tired."

They would make excuses for her, but they didn't need to, 'cause I loved her. As bad as she was to me, I still couldn't help but love her.

Then she started beating me. By the time I was nine, she got her motor skills back. She couldn't get all her words out, so she'd just punch me. Just full on. Because of her, I can take a punch like nobody's business.

I feel like I'm so strong in the chest area, mainly from her punches. I have always thought that's why my titties never grew. My sisters, all of them got titties. She punched mine down. Every day, I knew I was getting punched in the chest, slapped in the back of the head.

She liked to whip me with the bath brush, that you wash your back with. That's why I don't have one in my house now, because she liked to beat my ass with that wooden thing. She liked to get you right out of the tub, too. Soon as you got out:

Mom: "Didn't I tell you to wash the dishes?"

Tiffany: "I did wash the dishes."

Mom: "No, you didn't. You didn't wash nothing."

Tiffany: "Yes, I did. Yes I did."

It'd be like two dirty dishes that my sister had put in the sink after I'd washed the dishes. She'd just light my ass up.

When I was like ten or eleven, she would send me to school with all kinds of problems, like a busted lip or cuts or whatever. They'd call her up to school to get me, and the teacher's like:

Teacher: "Why's Tiffany's lip busted? What's going on with Tiffany? Did she have a fight or something?"

I didn't say anything. When the teacher asked me, I just didn't say shit.

Mom: "She's fine. She's fine. You know kids is clumsy. She just clumsy."

Then my mom started beating me on the bottom of my feet. I don't know if you ever been hit on the bottom of your feet, but you feel that through your whole body. You always pee on yourself, when somebody beats you on the bottom of your feet. Nobody should do that.

Then she became a super-crazy Jehovah's Witness, where she would talk about sex and then she'd be like, "We got to read the Bible now." One minute she'd be reading Bible scriptures, and you'd be feeling good and comfortable. And the next thing you know, she's snatching you by your hair, yelling, "Go wash these goddam dishes!" Go do this or that. You just never knew. "We have to go to church right now!" She'd drag your ass right off the bed at 4 a.m. to go to church, even though it was closed.

It was like living with a mean teenaged girl, who was hormonal and boy crazy. She used to talk to me about the weirdest things. I didn't understand it, but she would always talk about sex and stuff, like I was her friend. I guess because she didn't have any friends. After that accident all her friends fell off. She would talk crazy to everybody, because of the brain injury, and no one wanted to be around her.

She was boy crazy, but just for my stepfather. My mom was still having more kids. My baby brother Justin had just been born. She still was hooking up with my stepdad because she still said that's her husband, even though they were divorced now. She was fucking him in a Volkswagen.

At the time, I had no idea why he didn't come back to the house after the accident.

Then I found out, maybe.

For my twenty-first birthday, Step-Father took me out for

drinks. I was real depressed then. Around this time I had a break-down and I was physically ill. This was also the first time I got drunk. He had certainly had more than a few too.

Tiffany: "I don't know if I'm going to make it, man. I don't know if I'm going to live any longer. I know I'm twenty-one and everything, but I just don't feel like I'm going to make it, you know."

Step-Father: "Look, you are fine. You're going to make it. You're supposed to be here on Earth. God has a purpose for you."

Tiffany: "Man, God ain't got no purpose with me. I'm just God's punching bag. I feel like I'm a punching bag."

Step-Father: "Nope, you got a purpose, 'cause you're sup-posed to be dead. I'll tell you that right now. You and all your brothers and sisters. Y'all was supposed to be dead. Justin's not even supposed to be born. None of y'all sup-posed to be here."

Tiffany: "What do you mean?"

Step-Father: "Remember that car accident? You all was sup-posed to be in the car. I had a life insurance policy on all of y'all. I'm supposed to be a multimillionaire now, and y'all supposed to be gone."

He told me this whole story. That he took out all the insurance policies. Then he cut the line in her brakes. He said he knew that she drove too fast, and we was all supposed to be in the car that day. We was supposed to be dead.

That was the day that my mom left us all home, because I told her I could take care of the little ones. He said he hadn't planned for that, and that was the only reason it was just my mom.

He told me this.

I did not know what to say or do. I did not know if I was supposed to believe him or this was some weird fairy-tale horror story he thought would make me want to live. I was totally in shock. I had no idea how to take it. Later he would say that it was not true, he hadn't done any such thing. But it was too late to get it out of my mind.

After that, I started dating police officers. I started fucking police, trying to figure out how can I find out if this was real. And if it was, how can I get him prosecuted. How can I get him sent to jail?

But all the police were like, "Well, there's no way you can prove it. Where's the vehicle? It's just him saying it. He could have just been saying it to make you feel better when you were depressed. There's no way you can prove it in a court of law."

Fuck it. I didn't care. How much would it cost? I tried to get lawyers involved. I was dating lawyers, dating everybody, still trying to find out if this was real, if he should be prosecuted. But everybody said the same thing: "There's no way you can find out now. Too much time has passed."

It was pretty depressing. Had this man tried to kill us, ruined my mom's life, and for what? Or was he just so perverse that he had put this horror show into my mind thinking it would help?

You know what's funny? I could have set him up, if I really wanted to. Because he did it again. Years later, he asked me if I wanted my physically abusive ex-husband killed.

Step-Father: "Your sister told me what happened to you, with your husband. Do you want me to have this mother-fucker put to sleep? I can have him put to sleep. You know I was in Vietnam. I got motherfuckers that'll put him to sleep."

Tiffany: "Nah, I don't think you're really good at putting people to sleep. You're good at fucking up people's lives, but I don't think you're going to be able to put them to sleep because you didn't put my mama to sleep. I'm still awake. You're not good at that. I don't think so."

Step-Father: "All right. Well you let me know if ever you need me to put somebody to sleep. I ain't got nothing to lose."

So either way, this dude was messing with my head.

I try to forgive him. I really do try to find a place of forgiveness in my heart for him.

That shit is hard, though.

Foster Care

I was in foster care from the time I was thirteen until I was eighteen. We was taken from our mom when I was thirteen. I was moved around a lot in that one year. By the time I was fourteen, my grandmother got custody, but she kept us in the system so that she could have the money to raise us.

The reason I went into foster care in the first place was because my mom got in a fight, and she hit a baby with a two-by-four. For real.

It's a long, complicated story—as crazy family stories can be—but it boils down to this:

We had some neighbors that were all messed up, but my mom used to talk to the lady all the time. Her husband would always try to holler at my mom. One day, my mom got tired of the man and told him, "You leave me alone. Leave my kids alone." And they ended up getting in some kind of fight. Now mind you, this is after her accident, and she was mentally sick, of course.

When I got home from school, there was police everywhere. My mom was in the police car. The social worker was packing up my sisters' and brothers' clothes in trash bags. She told me to get a trash bag and put my clothes in the bag, 'cause my mom was not coming back home. That we gonna be placed in a foster home.

Tiffany: "Why are you all taking my mom away?"

Social Worker: "She got in a fight with the man, and she hit him with a two-by-four, and she accidentally hit his baby."

The baby was fine, but it caused all of this ruckus. The police showed up, and after talking to her, the police ended up taking her to the hospital, and diagnosing her. They gave her a 5150, so she had to be there for a seventy-two-hour hold. Then the doctors decided she's schizophrenic. They diagnosed her with that. She ended up being hospitalized for a year.

Step-Father was there, though. He showed up when I did.

Social Worker: "If he wants to take you guys, he could take you guys. At least take his biological children, and then I don't have to place them."

Step-Father: "Oh no, you take 'em. I don't have nowhere for 'em. You take 'em all."

So my mom went into a state mental facility for a year, and all my sisters and brothers went into foster care.

We didn't get to see my mom when she was in there. I remember we went to court one time and she was at court, and it didn't go well.

Judge: "You have to take your medications, you have to take a parenting class. You have to do all of that, it's the law."

Mom: "I don't need to do none of that by the law of God. Them is my kids, and y'all gonna give me my kids back."

She did not do any of those things, and so she did not get us back.

My grandma ended up taking the parenting class and doing what she had to do to get us. They wouldn't let her have us at first. I guess they felt like 'cause my grandma was there during that time that we were in danger, and she allowed us to be in danger, they didn't let us go to her right away. But, eventually, she got us.

But not before I had to spend almost two years in foster care.

I was in group homes for a while. Man, I hate thinking about that. It was more like a prison. I was only there for a while, but man, it was scary. That's when I started using my comedy skills, though.

My comedy came in real handy, because them bitches was out to beat my ass. We was in a dorm, like a big room and there's bunk beds everywhere. That's why I don't like bunk beds to this day. We was in there and these older girls was like:

Bully Girl: "Yeah you going to cry tonight, bitch, you're going to get your ass beat."

You ever seen *Saved by the Bell*? There's this episode where Screech puts his hand over his face, then he sticks his other arm through the crook of his elbow and punches with one arm while the other arm protects his face, but he looks all funky. So I started doing that, and they didn't know how to handle that.

Bully Girl: "Oh, this bitch is stupid. Is you stupid?"

So I started cracking jokes, and I'd bark like a dog. They started laughing, and then they started making fun of my hair.

Bully Girl: "You funny-looking, do anybody ever do your hair?"

Tiffany: "No, I got Raggedy Ann hair. This hair, you can't comb it. It breaks combs."

I thought that if I made these girls laugh, they wouldn't beat me up. They'd let me be the goofy one in the crew or something. But that didn't really work.

Bully Girl: "Yeah, they're about to lock these doors. When they lock these doors, that's it. You trapped in here with us."

Tiffany: "Oh yeah, we're going to be trapped? It's going to be like we in an Indiana Jones movie."

Bully Girl: "Ahhh bitch, we is still going to beat your ass . . . but you funny."

My social worker came and got me after two days and took me to a home. It was off of Normandy and 128th, which is the hood. This lady was so ghetto, but her house was so dope.

The first day I got there, she and my social worker were smoking weed and talking about me. They were sitting there, having a powwow in the living room, talking about me, getting high.

Foster Mom: "Well, is she fucking? Is she having sex? That's what I need to know."

Social Worker: "Well, she's thirteen."

Foster Mom: "That don't mean shit. Is she fucking? That's what I want to know."

Social Worker: "I don't think she's fucking. I'm pretty sure she's not fucking."

Foster Mom: "Hm, hm, you'd be surprised, these little kids be out here fucking. 'Cause you know the last one you had up in here, she was eleven years old, and I had to get her a whole box of condoms."

I was standing there, right in front of them, and they just talking all this shit. Then she decided to take me, and that was that.

She had her dad living with her, and she told us to call him Foster Grandpa. And he didn't have no teeth or nothing. He was kind of creepy, but he was nice. At least it seemed like it.

Foster Mom give me a tour of the house. "This is the bathroom you're going to be cleaning. This is the kitchen you going to be cooking in, 'cause everybody here contributes. This ain't no vacation spot. And here is the room you're going to sleep in. You see this drawer right here? This top drawer? It's full of condoms. Now, the Social Worker said you're not out here having sex, but who knows? Who knows? You probably are having sex, you just ain't telling nobody, right?"

And I'm just looking at her like completely confused. Of course I wasn't having sex!

This was when that movie *Crooklyn* came out, by Spike Lee. Foster Mom took me to see it, along with two other foster kids she was taking care of at the time. We went to that drive-in theater that was off of Centinela. We went to the drive-in movie theater, and the two little foster boys were in the backseat. They were giggling and trying to touch me. They was nasty little boys and I was pushing them off me. They were like eight and seven, right? The movie started and she went:

Foster Mom: "I know you're going to cry at some point, don't cry in my car."

Tiffany: "I ain't gonna cry."

She started blazing weed. Remember, this is in a car, and she had the windows up, so she was straight hot boxing us in there.

There was a man in the front seat with her, I can't remember who it was, some boyfriend of hers.

Foster Mom: "This is going to help you all to relax."

Boyfriend: "You know you crazy, right girl? You know?"

Foster Mom: "Man, these kids gonna be exposed to way more bullshit than this. You don't know what these kids been through. This ain't nothing. All y'all shut up and enjoy this movie."

I remember watching that movie and feeling like, *I know how this little girl feels.* I wanted to cry, but I didn't cry.

Then, when we was driving back, my eyes was burning and stuff, I guess 'cause I had a contact high, and I didn't even know it. Foster Mom saw me and said:

Foster Mom: "You know what, Tiffany? You seem like a really nice young lady, but I know you're out here doing things. I know you doing things. You probably gonna cry tonight, 'cause all that innocence is gone. It's all gone."

I didn't understand what she was talking about at all, not at that point. Still, I did cry a lot that night.

About a week later, I was doing my chores, and one of the little boys who was also staying with her came into the bathroom. He was butt naked with a condom on, talking about:

Foster Boy: "You wanna play with my dick? You want to play with my dick?"

Tiffany: "What the hell? What the hell is this?"

I freaked out and start running through the house, calling out to Foster Mom to get him.

Tiffany: "He out here naked! He out here naked!"

Foster Boy: "Stop being a snitch. Don't be a snitch. I'm gonna fuck your shit up."

Then she tried to blame it on me!

Foster Mom: "Oh, you tell this little boy to be naked like this?"

Tiffany: "I ain't tell that little boy to be naked. He's running around here with condoms on his dick. I don't know what that's about."

She slapped me in the mouth.

Foster Mom: "Don't be saying *dick*."

Really? This eight-year-old running around naked with a condom on, and she's worried about my language?

She told him to put on some clothes and stop playing.

The next day, that boy and the other boy started to make water balloons, right? Except all they had was condoms to make them with. Foster Mom was gone when they did this, and they started throwing these water balloons at me. Water-filled condom balloons.

I wanted to beat them up so bad, but I didn't. I just cleaned up the mess and threw all them condoms away. Threw out the condoms and told them to stop playing games.

She came back, and later that night, she found the condom drawer empty.

FosterMom: "Oh, you fucking, huh? How you fucking this many people that fast? What is you doing? Are you a ho?"

Tiffany: "No, I'm not a ho! They made water balloons. They was throwing them at me."

FosterMom: "Mm-hmm. Mm-hmm. Wait till I tell your social worker. Wait till I tell your social worker."

I guess she never told, 'cause nothing ever happened.

When school started back up, I was still living there. One day Foster Grandpa caught me in the bathroom, putting toilet paper in my little training bra I had.

Foster Grandpa: "What are you doing?"

Tiffany: "Ah, just putting some tissue in my shirt."

Foster Grandpa: "Why you doing that?"

Tiffany: " 'Cause all my friends, they got big boobs and I want to be like my friends."

Foster Grandpa: "Well I can help you make your titties grow."

Tiffany: "You can?"

Foster Grandpa: "Yeah, just let me suck on them every day. If you let me suck on them, they'll grow."

So, I started letting this old-ass man suck on my titties every day when I was thirteen.

He never tried to touch my cootchie or nothing. He just would suck on my titties for fifteen minutes before I left for school. Then I'd go to school.

When I was nineteen, I was hanging out with one of my girlfriends, and she was like:

Friend: "Yeah, I'm going to get a boob job."

Tiffany: "I don't know. I probably should get a boob job too, maybe."

Friend: "Or maybe we get somebody to suck on our titties every day until they grow."

Tiffany: "Oh that don't work."

Friend: "How do you know it don't work?"

Tiffany: " 'Cause I did that shit when I was thirteen years old."

Friend: "What do you mean, you did that when you was thirteen? I thought you didn't lose your virginity until you was like sixteen, seventeen?"

Tiffany: "I didn't, but this was different. This old man that was in my foster home, he would suck on my titties every day before I'd go to school, and it didn't do nothing. They didn't grow or nothing. They still the same size."

Friend: "Bitch, you was molested?"

Tiffany: "Wait, what?"

I had no idea I was molested. In my mind, "molested" meant somebody hurt you in some kind of way. Like, they took something from you that you didn't want to give. And what that old man did never hurt. It didn't necessarily feel good, either, it was just whatever. And he never tried nothing else with me, not even once. It was just like—in my mind—he was helping me out.

Look, *obviously* I can see now that this was messed up and absolutely was molestation. But at the time, I had no clue I was being molested. Even at nineteen, I had to have this pointed out to me.

I used to talk about it onstage all the time, 'cause parents say, "If somebody touch your private parts, or if somebody hurt your pee-pee, or if somebody pushed their private parts on you, you tell somebody."

But that man never did any of that. I never saw his penis. I never touched his penis. He never tried to make me touch him, and he never tried to touch my privates. He just sucked on my titties every day. And he wasn't even like, telling me not to tell anyone. I just never said anything, because I thought he was hooking me up. I thought he was helping me out.

I guess maybe we gotta update what we tell kids—that old men sucking your titties is *also* molestation.

Belonging

As a young kid, it didn't feel like nobody cared about me or protected me (except for my grandma). It didn't feel like anybody gave two fucks about me, unless it was benefiting them. Unless they was getting paid. Unless it was making them look good in some kind of way. Me just being myself was never good enough for anyone to love me.

My auntie Gina, she taught me how to dance. We would dance together, but that was so I could dance with her at weddings and make her look good. Having a little girl copying her moves. But I don't think it was because she loved me or liked to spend time with me or dance with me. That was just to make her shine.

My auntie Mary, she would do my hair. She would sing songs with me and stuff, but that was because she was rehearsing for her own thing. She'd be like, "Now, you do backups."

Now that I think about it, she was teaching me about music and performing, but really that was her getting ready for her own shit. It wasn't about me. It was about her looking good.

I didn't get much from my family, so I tried to be a gangbanger. But they wouldn't let me gangbang.

When I was a foster kid, I would have to walk through the gang hoods to get to the bus stop. I used to try to holla at all of them. I wanted to be in the gang, because I felt like then I'd be a part of something.

And I'd have me a man. Every gangbanger girl got a gangbanger boyfriend. You had somebody, that's what I wanted.

But it didn't work out like that. I couldn't get into the gang.

Gangbanger: "You too cute. You gonna be something one day. You can come and kick it, but you can't gangbang with us. If you want a drink or something, you can have a drink."

Tiffany: "I don't drink."

Gangbanger: "You don't even drink! Take your ass to school, bitch. Get the fuck up off the block."

Tiffany: "Let me hit the weed."

Gangbanger: "Your ass can't hit no weed. You don't know how to smoke, bitch. Go take your ass home and go read one of those heavy-ass books you got in your backpack."

They could cuss me out all the time, but I didn't mind. I just wanted to be a part of something, you know?

And the cool part was, I got to party with them, but didn't have to do all the terrible shit you have to do to be in a gang. Best of both worlds. Not a lot of shit went my way when I was young, but that did.

Grandma

Like I said, my grandma eventually got custody of me and my siblings when I was fourteen. I was still in the system, because even though my grandmother got custody of me, she wanted to get paid.

So we had to go to court and stuff. And the social worker came and checked on us every month and everything. We were with our grandmother, but we were still state property.

Even though my grandmother was my legal guardian, she didn't want to teach me to drive.

> *Grandma:* "I don't want to be responsible if you kill somebody. I'm not signing any paperwork."

I took the driver's ed class in school, and I did good.

I needed to be able to drive, because at that time I was making money as a hype woman for Bar Mitzvahs, and most of those were out where there wasn't many bus routes. So I had to get my social worker and a judge to sign that paperwork, for me to be able to get my driver's license.

I had the money to pay for the driving class and all of that, because of the Bar Mitzvahs. I remember my grandma was like:

> *Grandma:* "Oh you think you just so smart, huh? You just figuring out ways around everything, huh? You think you so smart."

> *Tiffany:* "Grandma, I'm going to be somebody. I'm going to be something, and I know I've got to have a car to do it."

> *Grandma:* "You got that right, you do."

I never understood my grandma. She would be so encouraging sometimes, and so mean at other times. I'd be like, *I don't know who this bitch is. I don't know if she here to help me or she here to hurt me.*

When I was eighteen, she put me out. She wasn't getting paid for me anymore, so she just put me out. I was just homeless.

Daddy

My first real memory of my daddy is when I was three and he head-butted my mom.

She was wearing one of those all-white jumpers like the girls had in the eighties, those sexy jumpers that women used to wear. I don't know why they were fighting, but I remember being on the couch and screaming loud and stuff and seeing blood. He head-butted my mom, and beat his own head, and blood was pouring down his face and her nose, and her white jumper was just covered with blood, all over.

Not too long ago, I asked my mom about this:

Tiffany: "Was that a dream that I had, that Dad head-butted you and your nose was bleeding?"

Mom: "No, you remember that?"

Tiffany: "Why was y'all fighting?"

Mom: "Because I threw hot water on him."

Tiffany: "Why did you throw hot water on him?"

Mom: "Because he came in the house at two in the morning, and he didn't give me the $300 he was supposed to give me, so I went in his wallet and I took the money. And then

I found another woman's number, and I called the number, talked to the lady, and then I boiled some water and threw it on him."

Tiffany: "You threw boiling water on him?"

Mom: "His skin wasn't burnt, I just wanted to get him to wake up."

My dad even admitted this when we briefly reunited.

Dad: "Yeah that happened. She stole my money, so I beat her ass."

I thought it was some crazy dream I'd had. I remember screaming so hard, till I couldn't scream anymore, you know like when a baby screams himself out?

Mom: "Yeah you pulled your hair out. There was blood, you had my blood on your face and your hair was missing."

At three, trying to make them stop fighting, I remember screaming until I pulled my hair out.

My dad is Eritrean. He abandoned me when I was three. I was reunited with my dad when I was twenty-seven. That's when I got married. He even came to my wedding. He was part of my life for a little while.

But then he just abandoned me again. It happened as I was working on this book. He was supposed to stay at my house. I flew him out, paid for him to be out here in LA. When he got here, I bought him all these clothes. All this stuff he wanted. Everything he asked for, I got it. Got him an iPhone 7, even.

Then I woke up on Monday, and he was just gone. He decided to take the Greyhound home. I called him:

Tiffany: "You know you had a plane ticket to go back to wherever you came from."

Dad: "No, I just decided to take the Greyhound, 'cause you made me feel like a pauper."

Tiffany: "How did I make you feel like a pauper?"

Dad: "Because, you think you're better than me!"

Tiffany: "When did I ever say I was better than you?"

Dad: "You walk around like you're better than me."

Tiffany: "What do you mean? Everything you asked for, I gave you. Anything you wanted, you had. How is that better than you?"

He hung up on me.

My friend told me that the answer to my question was right there, in his answers. He pointed out to me what he was trying to say, but couldn't say. This is what my friend said:

"He's ashamed of himself, because he left you when you were three, did nothing for you, and you ended up being very successful without him, and then you buy him stuff. You are not only a better person than he is, but you are kind and responsible where he is not, and you're providing where he did not. Not just as his child, but as a woman, providing for him. Your goodness holds up a mirror to his ugliness, and that is too painful for him, so he has to project this onto you, by saying you make him feel less about himself. It's nothing you did. It's guilt."

I don't get it. I don't get it, 'cause he's my dad, and whatever he asks for, he can have it. Isn't that what you're supposed to do for your parents?

I don't know. I just know that I was crying all day after he left. I was crying all day, because I just felt like that abandoned three-year-old girl again. I felt horrible.

All I wanted was for my father to be there with me. I didn't care about none of that other stuff.

Watch Yo Back

When I was twenty-three, I was staying at one of my grandma's properties. I told my grandma I'd take care of the property, so she'd let me stay there for free.

One day, I was getting ready to leave from the house to go to a party, and I had a cute little outfit on. All of a sudden, I heard this loud-ass knocking on the door.

It was my mama.

Mama: "Let me in the house. Let me in the house."

Tiffany: "I'm not letting you in this house."

Mama: "It's my mama's house. You let me in the goddam house!"

Tiffany: "I'm not letting you in this house, Mom. Like, you need to go somewhere. Go to Grandma's house, but I'm not letting you in this house."

Mama: "This is my mama's house! She own it!"

Tiffany: "I'm not letting you in. I'm about to go. I gotta go to an event, anyways."

I walked out the house with my short little skirt on.

Mama: "Where do you think you're going with that short-ass skirt? You trying to get pregnant out here? You out here being a prostitute?"

Tiffany: "No Ma, I was just going to an event, so leave me alone. Just leave me alone."

She had this long rearview mirror in her hand. Remember in the eighties, when they had them long, detachable rearview mirrors that had the smaller individual mirrors in it, which tilted to the sides? Somehow, she had found one of these mirrors. It was like two feet long. I could not understand why she had that in her hand.

I walked past her and said:

Tiffany: "I'm outta here, Mom. You need to leave, too. Get off the property."

Mama: "Oh, so you just think you grown now? You think you fucking grown?"

She reared back and threw that rearview mirror at the back of my head. It hit me. It hit me so hard in the back of the head, I just fell to the ground. Collapsed.

Mama: "That's right. You need to watch your back, bitch. Take that mirror with you and watch yo' motherfucking back."

I was looking so cute, I had on my little heels and everything, and it's just, BAM!

Tiffany: "I cannot believe you did that. I should call the police on you right now. I should call the police."

Mama: "Call the police, but just let them know that I got your back. I'm watching your back, bitch. Don't go out there getting pregnant."

Then, just as quick as she showed up, she left.

I had no idea what to do. So I just picked up the mirror and put it in my Geo Metro.

In my heart, I was so hurt and mad . . . but also I felt like that was so funny. Who throws a huge, broke-ass rearview mirror at people?

Sometimes I laugh so hard about it, but sometimes I just cry, because I know my mom is sick. She's sick, and she's trying to be a good parent, I think. In my mind, I like to think she was trying to be motherly, she was trying to tell me to be safe and not get pregnant. Trying to keep me out of trouble. You know?

But to this day, if I have words with somebody, I never walk past them. I never turn my back on them. Now I'm always watching people. I've never had that problem with somebody hitting me in the back of the head no more. Never again after that.

Mama

One time, when I was twenty-three, I got my tax return, and they gave me $4000 back. I told my mom:

Tiffany: "I'm going to spend a thousand dollars on you at the Walmart. I'm going to get you whatever you want at the Walmart."

I was doing it partially because she was my mom, but also because her mental illness was not going well. She was basically becoming a bag lady, carrying trash around.

But it was weirder than that. She would collect the trash, and she'd mail it back to the companies that manufactured it. She would say that's how she recycles and keeps the post office in business. That's how she would spend her disability checks, mailing trash back to the companies that it came from.

When you'd go into her apartment, she had five kids' car seats that she found. I don't know where she found them. And five piggy banks of the same type. My favorite character was Wonder Woman, so she had five Wonder Woman piggy banks, five Hello Kitty piggy banks. Like, five of whatever our favorite characters was as kids, for each one of my brothers and sisters. Five of everything, for each one of her kids.

Everywhere she went, she wanted to carry one of these bags of trash with her.

Tiffany: "Well, I'm going to take you to the Walmart. We gonna shop. Leave your trash at home. Leave it at home."

Mama: "It's not trash. It's not trash. This is recycling. I am helping the environment. I am removing my footprint. What are you doing for the environment?"

Tiffany: "I'm taking you to Walmart to buy you some stuff. That's what I'm doing."

We pulled up into the Walmart parking lot. She tried to take the bag of trash into the parking lot.

Tiffany: "Mom, you cannot take that into the Walmart. Leave it in the car."

Mama: "I'm not leaving it in the car, somebody might steal it."

Tiffany: "Mom, just leave this trash in the car. Just leave it here, and we'll come back for it."

Mama: "I'M NOT LEAVING IT IN THE CAR!"

She started yelling at me, and I don't do well with that. I just don't do well with people yelling at me.

I got mad and I snatched the trash and I tried to run to the dumpster. But before I could run to the dumpster, she snatched me by the back of my shirt and threw me up against the car and started punching me, repeatedly, in the chest and the stomach, in the mouth.

I started trying to fight her back, but she's crazy strong. She's five-foot-ten, two hundred and some pounds. Strong as shit. My little punches don't do shit. There's all these people walking by, and I started yelling, "Help! Help!" 'cause she is beating my ass and nobody is helping. They just looking.

She finally got tired of punching of me. I never did let go of that bag of trash, though. When she got tired, I just started jetting over to the dumpster, and I threw the bag of trash in the dumpster.

Once I got the trash in the dumpster, she tackled me and beat me up again by the dumpster.

Tiffany: "Mom, I just want to take you shopping with my money. This is crazy."

Mama: "Fuck you. I hate you. I hate you, Renee."

She started calling me Renee, which is the woman who my stepdad was cheating on her with.

Mama: "I hate you, Renee. I fucking hate you. I should kill you, but I'm not. I'm gonna let you suffer. I'm gonna let you fucking suffer."

She just walked away and went towards the Walmart. Like nothing happened.

At the front of the Walmart, there was a man in a wheelchair, the greeter. He's probably a veteran, and he's missing legs, and he's Mexican. He had one of those big mustaches and a Walmart shirt on, and he said, "Welcome to Walmart."

My mom spat on him.

Mama: "Your people make me vomit. I hate your burritos and everything. You make me vomit."

She hocked another loogie and spat in his face.

Once she spat on him, she continued to walk through the Walmart. Like nothing happened.

I was shocked. I tried to apologize to that man, but he was in shock, too.

Then and only then, did the police show up. They showed up immediately after that. Like, not even five minutes later.

I was getting my ass beat in the parking lot for forty-five minutes, and nobody came to help. But they immediately showed up when she spat on this Walmart employee.

The police came, and she started sprinting away from them, so they started chasing her. She ran out of the Walmart, into the actual mall, and they followed and chased her around the mall. It was crazy.

She is a big woman, and she was straight sprinting from the police. I didn't know what to think, except, damn, I did NOT know she could move like that.

They eventually caught her. I was following right behind them:

Tiffany: "That's my mom. Please don't hurt my mom. That's my mom. Please don't hurt my mom."

But she started struggling with them. It took six police to get her subdued. They had to hog-tie her. They tied up her ankles, and they made her legs connect like shackles, you know? Nobody wants to see their parents like that.

Mama: "Tiffany, this is all your fault. I could have been at my house, counting my shit. Tiffany, this is your fault. This is your fucking fault."

Tiffany: "Mama, it's not my fault. Why did you spit on that poor man?"

Mama: "I fucking hate you, Tiffany. I fucking hate you. This is all your fault. All your fucking fault."

They took her to the hospital. They ran her file and stuff.

Police: "Oh, she's a mental patient."

Tiffany: "She's not a criminal. I've been telling you this for an hour!"

Now remember, my lip was bleeding. My eyes were swollen, my ribs were hurting, and everything.

Police: "Who did that to you?"

Tiffany: "My mom did, but no, I do not want to press charges. I just want her to get help. She just needs help. She needs the right doctors."

She went into a mental institution then. She has been in and out, ever since.

Titus the Boyfriend

I've had some messed up relationships, but none were more fucked up than my time with Titus.

I met him in 2001, when I was coming back to LA from Daytona Beach. My friend Shamona and I had gone to the Black College Reunion, which was the new name for Freaknik (if you're young, you probably don't know what Freaknik is, and I'm not even sure if you can YouTube that shit, it was that long ago. So go ask some old person, and they'll tell you *all* about it).

I was waiting at the gate to board, and I looked at this guy who was watching a video with his homeboy. They had one of them old school handheld video cameras (this was before iPhones), and they were hunched together watching the tiny screen. I looked over their shoulders to watch, too.

The video was basically a black *Girls Gone Wild*. It was chicks shaking they asses and twerking, and the guys were smacking asses and grabbing booties, and all this stuff.

Tiffany: "Ooh, you guys had a good time, huh? Y'all had a blast."

They whipped around, looking scared, like they been caught . . . and then we all started laughing.

Now, let me pause real quick, and give you some background. Black College Reunion was like when all the salmon go upstream to spawn, and they squirting mating juices everywhere—that was basically Black College Reunion. Except with more DMX playing in the background.

But me and my friend Shamona, we thought we were better than that. We were the girls there who acted real uppity and classy. When dudes tried to talk about "Shake that ass!" we'd be like, "Ugh! Buy us drinks!" We were real snobby, talking about how we didn't do that stuff . . . but of course we *went* to Black College Reunion knowing what it was.

So we weren't any different, we just fooled ourselves.

I talked with them for a while, and as we were boarding, Titus saw me use my employee pass.

Titus: "Oh, you work for that airline?"

Tiffany: "Yeah, I work for them."

Titus: "Oh, that's crazy, I work for an airline too. Where you work at?"

Tiffany: "LAX."

Titus: "I work at LAX, too!"

Tiffany: "That's cool."

Titus: "Hey, you smoke weed?"

Tiffany: "No, I do not smoke weed. I don't do stuff like that."

Titus: "Oh . . . well, I do."

Tiffany: "How you smoking weed and working for the airline? They drug test me."

Titus: "There's ways to get around that."

That exchange basically sums up Titus. Sneaky and small-time.

Anyway, we talked all the way to LA. I remember in that first conversation, all the red flags were there. The dude lived with his mama, even though he was twenty-one and had a job! I should have run, but I was twenty and dumb.

We exchanged numbers, and we started talking and stuff. Just like friends or whatever. But basically, nothing was happening at all. So one day, I just laid it out.

Tiffany: "Look, I'm kinda talking to somebody. If you're not trying to be, like, my man, ain't really no reason for us to even be hanging out or whatever."

Titus: "What? We ain't even kissed or nothing!"

Tiffany: "Yeah, but I'm just saying. If you're trying to be my man, then you need to let me know, because I kinda like somebody."

And so then, he stepped it up a notch and took me on dates, and we started making out and shit. He introduced me to his mom, his sisters, the granny, everybody. I liked everybody, and they liked me. I introduced him to my siblings.

So we started being serious and being together all the time. We eventually got our work schedules matched up, so we'd be at work at the same time. Then we'd leave, we'd go places, and we basically did everything together.

He'd always be everywhere I went. He was around me so much, my cousins starting calling him "Tag-along." Other than that nickname, there ain't even anything funny or interesting to write about the first eight months of our relationship. It was a normal, early twenties relationship.

But then he met a pimp, and everything changed.

I can't remember his name, but he looked exactly like the rapper Suga Free. This pimp, Fake Suga Free, had two hoes. I remember the girls, too. They was nasty.

After Titus started hanging around him, one day we got to talking.

Titus: "You know, I could probably be a pimp."

Tiffany: "What? You ain't no damn pimp! You're a baggage handler!"

Titus: "I dunno. Fake Suga Free thinks I could do it."

Tiffany: "Why you hanging out with that guy? You're not a pimp, you're a baggage handler. And I like that about you. I like that when you come home from work, you smell like luggage. I like men who smell like their work. It means they have a job."

Titus: "Pimping is a job."

Tiffany: "I DON'T WANT MY MAN SMELLING LIKE A PACK OF HOES!"

Titus: "Yeah, but I could probably make more money pimping."

Tiffany: "Yeah, but you could also end up in jail. And what if you get, like, bad hoes? Then you'll lose money. It don't make sense."

He dropped it for a while. Then he got fired from his job with the airline.

Titus: "I'm finna go to full-time pimping."

Tiffany: "If you *finna* be a pimp, I'm *finna* be outta here."

Titus: "Okay, fine . . . I won't be no pimp."

So he got a new job working in a cosmetics factory, boxing makeup.

But he became real distant. We weren't hanging out all the time like we used to. For example, I would drop him off at work, and then I was supposed to pick him up. Then he wouldn't call me to pick him up, and I didn't know what he was getting up to.

And he would ask to use my car, which was fine. But then I wouldn't see him for two days.

Yeah, I know, I know. In retrospect, the signs were obvious.

What's funny is that it took a child to point them out to me. I mean literally an eight-year-old child.

One day, I was hanging out with Titus's mom and his sisters, and this one sister—who was, I repeat, EIGHT YEARS OLD AT THE TIME—spoke up.

Sister: "You know he cheating on you, girl. He cheating on you with this girl he met at the strip club. He pimping her in pornos."

Tiffany: "What? Titus ain't pimping nobody."

Sister: "Yes he is."

Tiffany: "You making this up."

Sister: "No I'm not!"

Tiffany: "Would you say that in front of your brother?"

Sister: "Yeah!"

So we got with Titus:

Tiffany: "What did you tell me about Titus?"

Sister: "That he cheating on you, girl. He cheating on you with this girl that he tried to get to be a stripper. Her name is Bertha."

Tiffany: "Bertha? How you gonna be a stripper with the name *Bertha*?"

Titus: "She lyin'! She don't know what she's talking about! She lyin'!"

I believed him. I didn't believe the little girl. I don't know why I didn't believe her, because she had nothing to lose by telling the truth. I was thinking maybe she was watching too much TV or something. Like I said, I was twenty-one and stupid.

Three months go by, and slowly things got worse. To the point where we were basically broken up, except not completely. You know how with some relationships, the breakup takes months to really get momentum and be real, but you know it's there long before? That's how it was.

It just so happened that I was scheduled to go on a cruise with my auntie. Titus had zero interest in that, until we were ready to break up, and I told him I wouldn't be seeing him for a week.

And now Titus wants to go on the cruise, too.

Titus: "Oh, you not going on a cruise, hell no."

Tiffany: "Oh I paid, I'm going on a cruise."

Titus: "No, y'all finna be on there hoeing."

Tiffany: "Are you crazy? I'm not hoeing with my auntie, she's twice my age."

He was really passionate about this idea that I was going on this cruise to get wild and hook up with a bunch of men. Yeah I know, he's projecting shit on me that he is doing behind my back. I can see that now, but I did not see it then.

The problem was that he didn't have any money to pay for the cruise. So, he got his mama to give him the money to get a ticket.

And get this: motherfucker comes on the boat with $50 in his wallet. For the whole weeklong cruise. The whole week with fifty bucks? Like, really?

The whole trip, he was just awful. Everywhere I went, if a man talked to me, Titus was all up in my business.

Titus: "Oh, you tryna holler at that dude? That man tryna get with you?"

It didn't matter if I was talking a ninety-year-old in a wheelchair with oxygen tubes, Titus would be trippin'.

Titus: "Oh you want some old ass now? That it? My dick is too hard for you now?"

Every few minutes, it was something. If I was dancing or having a good time, he'd come over.

Titus: "What you dancing for?"

Tiffany: "Because I like it, it makes me happy."

Titus: "Why you gotta be all happy?"

Tiffany: "It's a damn party, motherfucker! On a cruise! Why you think we're here, this ain't a fishing boat!"

Titus: "Oh, I see how it is, you lookin' to ride the Ho Boat to Ho Island!"

What's funny is that on that cruise I met the man who I would eventually marry, and then who would end up becoming my ex-husband. I had no idea at the time that any of this would happen. We just met a normal way. He said "Hi" or whatever, and we talked for a while. I wasn't even into him, but when he told me he was a policeman, I was like, *Oh, it's always good to have police friends.*

And then my future ex-husband starting acting weird, following me around the boat, filming me from a distance. And of course, Titus *hated* that, and he would yell at me about it, as the dude was lurking around, filming us.

What can I say? It was just all fucked up. But it gets worse.

The cruise was the week of September 11.

Of 2001. Uh-huh. THAT 9/11.

We were in Jamaica, and the Jamaicans started freaking out, talking about "Your Twin Towers are down!" Titus was all mad about that, too.

Once we got back to the boat, they were saying that all the airports were shut down. We were supposed to be back in the States the next day, but they were saying that nobody would be able to fly home. They let us stay on the cruise an extra four days, for $300.

Me and my auntie decided we would pay it and stay on the cruise. Titus couldn't afford to stay. Why not? Because he and his $50 was broke as hell, that's why!

I was *not* about to pay for him. He was so upset, so mad about that. He ended up having to sleep in the airport for a night, and the next day, he got to fly back to LA.

When we got back to LA, we were still together, but not really. On the one hand, we were breaking up, but just couldn't seem to actually do it. On the other hand, I still thought I was going to marry him, and I thought I could trust him. I felt this way even though he would take my car and say, "Oh, I'm just going to go to the store and I'll be right back." And he would be gone for, like, twenty-four hours.

I just figured he was with his friends or whatever. I didn't need the car, because I was at work, anyway. You know?

It didn't really dawn on me that he would be with somebody else, because I thought he loved me.

Then I found out I was pregnant. I didn't know what to do.

So I freaked the fuck out.

This whole pregnancy thing made me feel like such a loser. I felt so stupid. I still had all these dreams and goals for myself that I wanted to accomplish, and here I was knocked up by this broke-ass loser.

It made me really look at the big picture. I was just barely living in this little studio apartment. Titus was living with his mama. Titus didn't even have a car or a job. He just came on a cruise with $50 on him. How are we going to raise a kid? I only make $400 a week at my job, and then with the Bar Mitzvahs, I'm clearing $2500 a month. That's not enough to raise a kid.

I can't have no baby by this man. I can't even be with him. *I don't even like him anymore.*

When I first told him, he wanted the baby.

Titus: "Yeah, that's right. That's mine."

Tiffany: "What the fuck are you talking about? How we gonna pay for this? You ain't got no job!"

Titus: "It's all right, baby, that's why they got welfare. We be aight."

Tiffany: "Is you fucking retarded? I'm not going to be no welfare mom!"

I did not want to have an abortion, but at the same time, I did not want to have a baby with that man, in those circumstances. What kind of life would that be for the baby?

What if something happened to me? This man couldn't even take care of himself, how was he going to take care of a child? If I died the kid would inherit what? A Geo Metro? That's not a good inheritance.

And honestly, I was not ready to be a mom. I hadn't even gotten to experience life at this point. How could I raise a child, you know?

I felt the weight of the world on me. I felt like if I had this baby, it'd be the biggest mistake of my entire existence.

I felt terrible, I felt like I was going to go to hell for this. But you know what? I'd rather go to hell and die without a baby on Earth, suffering, than have a baby here on Earth that suffered. That ain't right.

We were still arguing about it, then he took my car to go pick up some food for us . . . and he didn't come back for two days. Then he walked in.

Titus: "You should probably go ahead and take care of that."

On the way to the clinic, he was trying to shame me. You know how when somebody's like, they want you to do something, but they don't want to feel bad about their role in it? They want you to take the blame for it, so they don't have to feel bad about themselves?

Titus: "If you don't want to do this, you don't have to. It's all on you. You want to kill my baby, that's on you."

I fucking hated him right then.

I remember the clinic so vividly. As I walked through the door, something came over me. I hate to admit this, but it's true—I became very happy.

It was like a total one-eighty from how I felt in the parking lot to how I felt once I went through that clinic door. I felt like I was doing the most responsible thing in the world. I just felt really, really joyous. I knew, as painful as it was, this was the right thing.

You go into a room, then they put you on this bed. I was smiling the whole time. This one lady, this Hispanic lady notices.

Hispanic Lady: "Why are you so happy?"

Tiffany: "I guess because I know that I'm not going to be in this trap. I know I'm not going to be in the trap anymore."

She just smiled back and rolled her eyes.

They put you to sleep for a little bit, for like ten minutes, and do the procedure. Then when I woke up, I reached down between my legs, and I felt the big ol' maxi-pad thing they put on you.

I jumped out the bed, and I started to dance. I started full-on dancing.

Nurse: "Ms. Haddish, you can't dance. Ms. Haddish, you are scaring people!"

Tiffany: "I'm free!! I'm free!! Thank God almighty, I am free!!"

I started doing the Running Man, and then I ran my ass right into the ground. Those drugs they give you are strong.

They made me sit down and act calm. I looked over and there was a Mexican lady, she was awake and looking at me like I fucking lost my mind. Then there was another girl in the room, and she was just full-on crying. Here I am just as happy and joyous as can be. I kinda felt bad about my dancing, and I was chill after that. Not everyone was happy about being there.

When I walked out, I was just smiling. I'm like a little doped up and kind of woozy or whatever, but I'm really happy. I'm like genuinely happy. Titus was so mad that I was so happy.

Titus: "So you just joyous, huh? You just joyous?"

Tiffany: "Yeah, we don't have no stress no more. There's no stress. We got a second chance."

Titus: "That's all right. I'm going to just get you pregnant again in two months. You're just going to be pregnant again."

Little did he know, I had gotten a Depo shot when I was in there. I didn't even tell him. This man was not trapping me again.

Things actually got cool again for a few weeks. It seemed to be getting better. He's not disappearing. Then my birthday came up, and he said he needed my car, because he was going to an interview.

Tiffany: "Okay. But it's my birthday."

Titus: "Yeah, I'm going to take you over to my grandma's house, use your car, go to my interview. I'm going to come back, and we're going to go out."

He didn't come back until the next day.

Tiffany: "Yo, what happened? No call, no nothing? Where were you?"

Titus: "I had got caught up in some stuff, but it's all good. I'm going to take you out today."

Tiffany: "I got to go to work. This is so stupid. I don't get it. Why would you even do that? You just ruined my birthday. You ruined my birthday."

Titus: "Stop tripping. You're tripping. Just relax. I'm going to make it up to you."

Three days go by. I go over to his house—which is his mom's house, 'cause he don't have his own place. I was ready to forgive him. I don't know why I was, but I was. And most importantly, I was now healed up from my abortion, and we can have sex again, for the first time since I was dancing for joy.

I went in his room, and I saw he had a video camera on his TV. I don't know why, but I had this weird feeling come over me.

Tiffany: "Let's do something freaky. Let's make a movie."

I grabbed the video camera, and I started recording. He immediately got all mad, snatched the camera from me, scratching my face in the process.

Titus: "You need to mind your motherfucking business!"

Tiffany: "What is wrong with you? What's on that tape where you got to be acting like that?"

Titus: "Ain't nothing on this motherfuckin' tape. You just need to mind your motherfuckin' business and stay out my shit!"

I tried to reach for the camera, and he snatched it away. He took the tape out the camera, went out the house, and threw it in the dumpster.

I knew. All of it dawned on me, right then in that moment. Not like, consciously, but I knew. I felt it in my body.

Was I smart enough to admit that shit to myself in the moment? Hell no! I just said to myself, *You need to just chill. You love this dude. You need to chill.* I still didn't know that I should listen to my gut and my feelings and my body.

When he came back in the house, I decided to change up. I just started being real sweet and nice, and we started kissing and stuff.

Tiffany: "I just want you to hook me up. I want to get me some head."

So he went down on me and gave me some head. Once he was done, he was all hard and ready to penetrate me. He was literally right about to put it in, and I mean like, an inch before his penis touched me, I pulled away. My body was screaming at me, and not in a good way.

Tiffany: "Ooh, wait. No. I got to go to the bathroom. I got to boo-boo."

I sat in the bathroom for like thirty minutes. I was crying, because it all hit me at once.

I knew everything was true. His sister was right. I could just feel it in my bones. I was talking to myself, *Oh God, everything she said is true. I'm so stupid.*

This man was betraying me so much right now. A feeling of disgust for him came over me. I was disgusted by him, and I felt disgusted for myself for being so blind. You know?

I was crying so much. You know how you do that quiet crying, like the tears are coming out and you're breathing hard, but you don't want nobody to hear you crying? I remember I was just covering my face, just trying to hold it together, tears running through my hands.

And quite frankly, the head was not good. It wasn't. It was, like, the worst.

Eventually, he came banging on the door.

Titus: "You all right in there? What the hell?"

So I started making throw-up noises, acting like I was puking. I was just so disgusted with him, I needed to find a way out.

Tiffany: "Man, I'm sick. I'm not well. I need to go home. I'm going to go home, all right? I'm so sick. I cannot function right now."

I left. I got in my car. It was raining bad. I got in my car, and I started full-on crying. Like, heaving sobs, makeup-stained tears running down my face, all that shit.

I pulled myself together, and I started to drive off. I got down to the street, and all of a sudden I was like, *What the fuck was on that damn tape? What the fuck was on that tape? I need to know what the fuck was on that tape.*

I parked a block away, and walked in the rain back to his place. My hair was fucked, but I gave zero fucks at this point. I broke into the apartment building that he lived in with his mom. I hopped over this gate and jumped into the dumpster. I was diving in that dumpster for like an hour looking for that tape.

And I found it.

I was so dirty. I just remember feeling like a piece of shit. I felt like garbage—I literally had actual garbage all over me—but I had to find out what the hell was on this tape.

This was one of those mini-videotapes, and I needed an adapter to play it on my VCR. Once I had the tape, I drove around for about three and a half hours looking for an adapter. I drove all the way to Orange County, still smelling like garbage, trying to get one, but no one had it.

I bought a pack of cigarettes. I didn't even know how to smoke. I went home, and I smoked like three cigarettes. I was going, *I hope this kills me right now.* I have no idea why I thought three cigarettes was going to kill me, but I did. That's how fucking loopy I was right then.

At 5 a.m., I called my friend Anna. Her work involved some kind of media stuff, and I remembered she had the same kind of video camera as Titus had.

Tiffany: "Can I borrow your camera?"

Anna: "What do you need it for? What's going on? It's 5 a.m., what you need a video camera for? You murder someone?"

Tiffany: "I just need it."

Anna: "Why do you sound like that?"

Tiffany: "I just smoked cigarettes."

Anna: "Why are you smoking cigarettes?"

Tiffany: "This motherfucker scratched my face, and I found his videotape in the dumpster and I just hope I die."

Anna: "What does that have to do with cigarettes? What is going on?"

Tiffany: "Anna, look . . . you want weed? I'll get you some weed if you let me borrow that camera."

Anna: "Okay, yeah. Bring me some weed, and I'll bring my camera."

I got the weed and went over to Anna's. I guess I was in worse shape than I realized.

Anna: "Tiffany, you need to calm down. You should probably hit this weed."

Tiffany: "Fuck the weed. I just need that video camera. I need to go home and watch this tape."

Anna: "Tiffany, I ain't givin' you the camera till you hit the weed and have a drink. You need to relax."

She opened a bottle of Cisco. It was peach Cisco, because we classy. We sat there, 7 a.m., smoking weed and drinking peach Cisco. Then I calmed down a lot.

I went home and plugged the video camera into my TV. Oh man, it was so bad. Lemme try to explain it.

It's that girl, Bertha, that his sister told me about. It starts out with them talking.

Bertha: "I'm better than your girlfriend, Tiffany. I can do everything better than her. She's not all that. You always talking about her like she's so special, but she's not special."

Titus: "She is special. But I'm going to have to teach you how to do it better, because you're not making me enough money. I'm going to teach you how to suck a dick right."

Bertha: "Okay. Show me how to suck your dick right."

Titus: "Now, when Tiffany sucks my dick . . ."

I just started bawling out of control.

The whole tape was "Tiffany does it this way" and "No, when

Tiffany do it, she don't do this. She do this." And she was all into it, "Does Tiffany do this? Does Tiffany do it like this?"

I cried hard. For a long time, I just cried and cried. I cried until I cried so much that I got fucking dehydrated. I cried all the fucking water out of my body.

Then I started to get pissed. I realized this motherfucker is giving this bitch all my fucking tricks. Ain't that some bullshit?

Then he started fucking her. And he's fucking her without a condom.

And my birthday is time-stamped at the bottom of the fucking video.

I wasn't crying no more. I started screaming at the TV. I was screaming at the TV like some crazy woman, I was so mad.

And that bitch's face. Oh hell no. You ever see them chicks that got the big gums and little baby teeth? That was her. That old dog-mouth bitch was staring at me as she got fucked by my man, on my birthday.

I watched it probably about four times. I called him.

Tiffany: "I'm done with you. This relationship is over. I'm not fucking with you no more. I fucking hate you. You a dog, nasty, dirty-dick motherfucker. You ain't shit."

I was just going in on him, right? For, like, fifteen minutes, I used every curse word and bad thing I could think of. I didn't let him get a word in, I didn't listen to shit he said, I just went in on that motherfucker.

A few hours later, he showed up at my house. He walked in and saw the tape playing.

Titus: "How did you get that tape?"

Tiffany: "How you think I got it, you dumb motherfucker?"

Titus: "You fucking crazy. You a crazy bitch going in the trash like that. That shit is garbage."

Tiffany: "You best get the fuck out my house, before I commit murder."

Titus: "Oh come on Tiff, that doesn't mean anything. I was teaching her. I was teaching her."

Tiffany: "Nah, you a fucking cheater. You a liar. Your sister was right."

He was thinking he would take the tape from me when he came over there. HELL NO! I hid that shit, then I called the police.

Tiffany: "You best to get out of here. The police coming."

That phrase will scare off any black guy (except Obama . . . *maybe*). He left so fast, he didn't even get his clothes and shoes and other stuff he had left at my place.

Once he left, my anger subsided, and the sadness came back. I was just devastated. This hurt so much.

He kept blowing up my phone. I ignored him. Then he got his mama, his grandmama, his aunties, all these people in his family to start calling me. They laid the guilt on thick, telling me that "You destroying him. He loves you so much. He's so depressed. He can't function without you."

I never told them that he cheated on me or that he made this sex tape or anything like that. I don't know why. As much bad as he'd done to me, I just didn't want to do that. I knew how much they put him on a pedestal. They really loved him. I didn't want to destroy that.

But they kept bothering me about him, making me feel like it was my fault. I *know* he didn't tell them about all the shit he'd done to me. Then Anna pointed out some real obvious shit that I'd missed.

> *Anna:* "Why you lettin' him hide his dirty shit? You should make everybody in that family fucking pay. They knew about that bitch. If the *little sister* knew, they ALL knew. They knew what the fuck he was doing. They knew."

She was right. They had to know. Ain't no way the only person in the family to know the truth is some eight-year-old girl.

I devised a plan. Oh, it was so fucking devious. It was straight-up evil . . . but that motherfucker, and his family, deserved it.

First I got about fifteen bootleg copies of that movie *Charlie's Angels*. It had just come out. Anna's boyfriend was a bootlegger, and he helped me make some . . . alterations . . . to the movie.

I made copies for all the family members who called my phone, all of them that called me and was telling me, "He love you. You're doing him wrong." Christmas was coming up, so I wrapped them up real nice, and I sent all fifteen copies to his family members as gifts.

Then I ate a lot of corn. A lot. And I didn't chew it so well. And I made a different present for him.

Once it was ready, I called him.

Tiffany: "I was tripping. I love you. I can't live without you. You're like the best thing that ever happened to me. I can't be without you. I really want to be your girl. I just need you to stop messing with that chick."

Titus: "I'm going to leave her alone. No problems. I wasn't making no real money off of her anyways. Fuck the pimp life. I'm not going to live that life. I'm not doing it no more. It's just me and you."

I went over to his house, and I brought his shoes and other stuff back to him.

Tiffany: "Babe, we should, for our first thing together, let's go play basketball. We should play basketball."

Titus: "Bae! That's what I'm talking 'bout!"

He was about to put on some regular shoes, and I stopped him.

Tiffany: "Nah, you should put on your Jordans, the ones you had at my house. You'll be the freshest dude. You'll be the shit on the court. You'll be killing them out there. Put these on. If you're my man, you're going to be the finest dude out there."

Titus: "All right. All right. I like this."

He put his foot in the shoe.

Titus: "What the fuck? What's in this shoe?"

He pulled his foot out and there was shit all over his foot.

And the shit was full of corn.

Titus: "What the fuck? Somebody shit in my shoe! Is that human shit?!? There's corn in it!"

Tiffany: "Yeah, all the shit you put me through, NOW YOU WALKING THROUGH IT, MOTHERFUCKER!!!"

I took off running out of the apartment, because I figured he might try to do something. When you ruin a black man's shoes, you never know what's going to happen.

But then I stopped running. I realized he wasn't going to do anything. Besides being a coward—which he was—he was not about to track shit all through his mama's house, right?

Once I got outside, I could hear him yelling, screaming from his balcony, being all hysterical.

Titus: "YOU A DIRTY BITCH!! YOU A NASTY, DIRTY BITCH!!"

Later that day, his mom called me.

Mom: "Why would you shit in his shoe?"

Tiffany: "I hate your son. I fucking hate him. I mean, I love him, but I hate him. He's a fucking loser. He's a shitty-ass motherfucker. He wanna drag me through shit? Then he can walk in it, too!"

Mom: "Girl, you fucking crazy. Something wrong with you. You have a mental problem."

Tiffany: "I didn't have no mental problem until I met your raggedy-ass son."

Mom: "And he got shit all over my carpet, how am I going to clean this up?"

Obviously, that broke us up for good.

But my master plan was not over. There was one more chapter.

Christmas Day came. I was at work at the airlines, at the ticket counter. My white manager came up to me.

Manager: "Tiffany, there is a woman on the phone for you. She is very angry. She sounds black, and she is . . . very, very angry. I don't normally like employees taking personal calls on shift, but she is, well . . . she is very insistent that she talk to you."

I already knew who it was, and what it was about.

Tiffany: "Hello?"

Mom: "MY CHILDREN SAW THAT!! WHAT IS WRONG WITH YOU! MY CHILDREN SAW THAT!!"

It was Titus's mom. Remember the fifteen *Charlie's Angels* VHS tapes I sent out to all of his family for Christmas?

I had Anna's bootlegger boyfriend splice in the porn that Titus shot with Bertha, right into the middle of the movie.

He even made up a little title card that said "Titus's Angel" that cut right to him fucking her.

Oh *hell* yes, I went there.

Mom: "WHY YOU PUT THAT FILTH IN MY HOUSE?!"

Tiffany: "WHY YOUR SON FUCKING AROUND ON ME WITH SOME HORSE-MOUTH HO?!?! ON MY FUCK-ING BIRTHDAY!! WHAT'S UP WITH THAT???"

Then his grandmother took the phone from her.

Grandmother: "Oh my God, girl! You got my grandbaby dick out. I done had a seizure. I got these kids up in here watching *Charlie's Angels*, and then all of a sudden, you got my grandson on here fucking this bitch."

The whole family—it was like the kids, grandkids, everybody—sitting there watching. His whole family saw that shit. They all saw what a fucking lying cheater he was, they all saw them big gums and those tiny teeth. They saw it all. I was tired of being framed as the bad girlfriend, when I wasn't. Titus couldn't hide no more.

Then I heard his auntie in the background.

Aunt: "My nephew got a big ol' dick."

Grandma: "I should beat your ass. You better bring me every copy of that tape you got. Oh my God. You better not put my grandbaby dick on no Internet. I will sue you, bitch. I will have you killed, if you got my grandbaby dick out here like this."

Best revenge ever, right?

That was the end of my relationship with Titus and his family.

But the fallout was not over. Oh, no. In some ways, it was just the beginning.

Because Titus tried to be a pimp (and failed), I ended up actually becoming a real-life pimp, but that's another story altogether.

The Pimp Gets Pimped

The day after the *Charlie's Angels* Christmas, Bertha called my house, looking for Titus.

Bertha: "Hi. My name is Bertha, and I'm looking for Titus."

Tiffany: "Titus don't live here."

Bertha: "Well, he calls me from this number sometimes. I can't find him. He's been missing for a couple of days."

Tiffany: "He's been missing? Oh, you that bitch, ain't you?"

Bertha: "Are you Tiffany? Oh, it's so nice to hear your voice. I hear so much about you. He's always talking about you. You're such a nice person."

Tiffany: "Oh no, bitch. I'm not nice. Just ask Titus how nice I am."

Bertha: "I don't know why you're so angry at me. I just work for him."

Can you believe this? I kept talking to her, and I started realizing this bitch is dumb as fuck.

Tiffany: "Oh, what kind of work do you do for him?"

Bertha: "Well, you know, like customer service–type work."

Tiffany: "Customer service–type work? Girl, keep it one hundred, because I remember him saying he wanted to be a pimp. So you a ho?"

Bertha: "I'm *not* a ho. I'm an entertainer."

She told me about how she met Titus through his homeboy or whatever, and that she wanted to be in movies. She wanted to make money, and they told her that she could make money being in movies having sex with people, so that's what she'd do.

Tiffany: "So how much money are you making doing entertainment?"

Bertha: "None, because he keeps all the money. But he gets my hair done, my nails done. He buys me clothes. He feeds me."

I know, right? To be honest, though, I didn't have no place calling her a dumb bitch. I let that motherfucker lie to me too, just about different shit.

I told her Titus wasn't ever coming back to my place, so she didn't need to call me again. Then the next day, she called me.

Bertha: "Oh, you a nasty, dirty bitch! You shit in his shoes? You nasty, dirty bitch!"

I guess she found Titus.

Tiffany: "No, *you* the nasty, dirty bitch. You're the one that's out here fucking random motherfuckers on camera. And you don't got money to show for it!! You giving your pussy up for nothing."

We was going back and forth arguing with each other over who was the nastiest, dirtiest bitch. Eventually, it came down to what all black women arguments come down to:

Bertha: "I should come beat your ass!"

Tiffany: "I wish you *would* come try to beat my ass."

Then she told me my address. That nigga told her where I live?

Bertha: "I've been in your house before. I've been in your car. I've been in your bed."

Boy, I was fucking HOT. I hung up the phone and went to go see my girl Anna. She flipped it on me.

Anna: "Stop arguing with that bitch and start fucking working that bitch. She's stupid, so use it to work that bitch."

Tiffany: "I don't even know what that means, Anna."

Anna: "You just as dumb as her! Listen, be nice. Turn her against him. Take his ho from him. Without no ho, he ain't no pimp."

I thought about that shit all night. The next day, I called Bertha.

Tiffany: "Hey, I'm not calling to argue with you or anything. I totally get what I did was kind of out of order or whatever, but really, I don't want no beef or no problems."

Bertha: "That's nice to hear, thank you, Tiffany."

Tiffany: "I've been thinking about what you said, and I just want to know. How are you out here giving up your body and not making any money off of it? It just don't make no sense to me."

We started talking, and I asked her a bunch of questions.

Tiffany: "You doing these pornos. How much are you getting?"

Bertha: "I don't know what I'm getting paid, because he takes the money."

Tiffany: "Girl, I could probably hook you up with some gigs, and I would just take 10 percent."

Bertha: "Really?"

Tiffany: "Yeah. If you made $1000, I would only want $100. If you made $1500, I would just want $150."

Bertha: "Hmm. This sounds like it would be a good thing."

We started talking on the phone every day, and I kept working her. So now I was on the phone with her for about a week and a half, two weeks. She done became my friend. Right? I was like, I hate her though. I fucking hate her.

Tiffany: "I'm telling you. You could make a lot more money, if you just work with me. You could even still be with him. He could be your man or whatever y'all got going on, but you should work with me."

She agreed, so I started looking in the *LA Weekly*, and I found her a gig to do like three porns. I got her $1500 for one, $700 for another, and the other one, she had to get fucked in the ass and her pussy by two dudes, so I got her $1800 for that. I took her to the sets, she fucked, I got my cut, and I gave her the rest.

Bertha: "This the most money I ever had. Oh my God. Thank you so much, Tiffany. Thank you so much!"

Then I had another friend who was a stripper, and I had her show Bertha some moves. I helped her go from $70 a night to $300 or more. And I got my cut from that, too.

One day, Titus made her mad, and she dropped it on him:

Bertha: "You're a fucking horrible pimp. Tiffany is a way better pimp than you'll ever be."

Titus: "What?"

Bertha: "Tiffany is a way better pimp than you'll ever be. She's a great person."

Titus: "What the FUCK are you talking about?"

Bertha: "Tiffany's been taking me to do pornos. See all this money I got?"

Even better—she did this in front of his homeboys, who were actual pimps.

Pimp Friend 1: "Damn, Titus! Yo bitch took yo bitch?"

Pimp Friend 2: "Maybe Tiff should hang with us. She sound like the true pimp."

He called me, all hysterical, voice trembling.

Titus: "You take my bitch?"

Tiffany: "Yeah, I took your bitch, BITCH, and I'll do it again. I'll take all your bitches, you little dirty-ass mother-fucker."

Titus: "I fucking hate you. You're a horrible person."

I just felt so good. I felt like I really accomplished a lot.

Eventually, I started pimping Titus's *male friends*. One of his boys— we called him Goliath because he was so huge—heard what I had been doing for Bertha. He asked me if I could set him up, too. I started off getting him some pornos, and those went well. Then something else came up.

I was still doing Bar Mitzvahs on the weekends, and of course, if you're doing Bar Mitzvahs, you're going to meet old Jewish ladies. I met a lot of lonely ones, and I got to be friends with them. Then they started telling me how lonely they were and saying things like, "My husband's not satisfying me."

I remember the first conversation that started it. I had just finished a Bar Mitzvah practice, and was about to leave.

Jewish Lady: "No, Tiff. Stay. Have a glass of wine with me. I don't really have a lot of friends. My husband has all the friends. I don't really have anybody to hang out with. It's kind of lonely in this big old house."

I thought this was kind of weird, but this was a rich lady, so whatever. I'd talk to her. She did seem lonely. She was telling me about how her husband's never at home, how her sex life was down the drain.

Jewish Lady: "I feel like I'm a virgin again. He doesn't touch me or anything."

Tiffany: "Oh, wow."

Jewish Lady: "So who are you dating? I bet you date hot guys."

Tiffany: "I do okay."

We had this same conversation, like, three times, until I finally got fed up.

Tiffany: "Girl, why don't you just buy some dick? You should come with me to the strip club and just check it out."

Jewish Lady: "Oh, no. I couldn't be seen in a place where men are dancing."

Tiffany: "Well, just buy some. They won't tell nobody. Just keep it on the down low."

Jewish Lady: "On the down low?"

I straight up had to play some R. Kelly, "Down Low" for her, to explain what that meant.

She gave me this crazy look, like a kid that stole candy.

Jewish Lady: "I've never been with a black guy. I would love a strong black man. What's it like doing a black guy?"

Tiffany: "Well . . . they be smelling like cocoa butter. That's nice. They be all strong, and they dicks are so powerful. If you find a man with an ass, oh my God. It's just so good. They pick you up. It's just good. It just depends on who you get with, though. But they can be good."

Jewish Lady: "That's what I need."

Tiffany: "But you know, any guy could be really great, if you guys have a connection and stuff."

Jewish Lady: "I don't need the connection. I'm married. I just need to have an orgasm. I just want to feel ravaged."

She started showing me these romance novels she had. All her romance novels were like, I don't know. She had one that was like a slave thing or whatever. It was a big, strapping black guy on the cover, holding this passed-out white woman.

Tiffany: "Well, I don't know any slaves, but I could probably hook you up with somebody big and strong."

So I hooked her up with Titus's boy, Goliath. She'd give me $200, I'd take $50, give the rest to Goliath, and then set up the meeting.

Then she introduced me to another lady. I linked her up with another guy that was a friend of Goliath. It was kind of like word of mouth, and I started having a lot of clients.

One lady wanted a strong white man. I didn't know any huge white guys, but I used to be in Venice Beach a lot, and I met this dude on the boardwalk.

Tiffany: "Hey, would you ever fuck for money?"

Big White Dude: "Yeah. Of course."

Just like that. Pimping dudes was easy.

The problem was that I wasn't really necessary. A lot of these guys, once I introduced them and got my $50, they started hooking up with these chicks on their own, doing their own thing.

Which makes sense, to be honest. Aside from the intro, they didn't need me.

So I ended up getting out of pimping, because I didn't make much money. It's just not a lucrative business, selling dick. Dick ain't really all that hard to come by.

Roscoe the
Handicapped Angel

In my early twenties, I worked the ticket counter at an airline. When you checked in to your flight, I was the girl who printed your ticket and tagged your bags.

Roscoe was my baggage handler. He would stand behind me at the counter and throw the bags on the conveyor belt.

Roscoe was also handicapped. And not just a little handicapped; dude was messed up in multiple ways.

To start with, he only had one working arm. I don't know how he even got that job—who hires a baggage handler with only one working arm?

His right arm was big and strong and it worked great. But his left arm was like, this tiny deformed little arm. It was permanently bent at an angle, and kinda hung there and looked like a T. rex arm. He could move the fingers and stuff. Otherwise, it couldn't do much. Like a baby arm that never fully developed.

It made me feel creepy at first. Have you ever seen a physical deformity on a person, and at first, it sends a chill down your spine? Even if you don't want to feel that way, you do. For the first few weeks, I was straight-up repulsed by that dead baby arm. Eventually, I moved on to sympathy, "Oh, poor Roscoe." And then after that, I was just used to it, and treated Roscoe like anyone else.

His arm wasn't the only thing off about him. His face was always making crazy expressions. You ever seen someone who had a stroke and couldn't really control their face afterwards? It was like that. I don't know if he actually had a stroke or if he was born that way, but his mouth went to the side, and it made him talk mush-mouthed.

It took some time to get used to how he spoke, because his mush-mouth made him draw out all his vowel sounds and for real made him sound slow. He said my name like it was three different words: "Tiff-a-Knee."

But he was *not* mentally disabled. You could have a normal conversation with him, and he would totally be able to talk to you. At times, he was even smart. And man, he was funny. You can't be funny if you're dumb.

But mainly, he didn't give a fuck. I remember one time soon after I met him, I had this one customer who was *such* a bitch. She was complaining about every little thing, cussing her husband out, trying to yell at me. I kept being nice, because that's how they trained us, but she was being a straight-up bitch. When she walked away, Roscoe came up behind me:

Roscoe: "Wow, whatta fuckin' bitch. I hope she getta yeast in-fec-shuuun, dat stoopid bitch."

Tiffany: "What'd you say, Roscoe?"

Roscoe: "She stoopid talkin' to youuu like dat, Tiff-a-Knee. She can't be talkin' to youuu like dat. Fuckin' bitch."

Tiffany: "Roscoe, you can't talk like that at work!"

It was even more shocking coming from him, because I kind of assumed that handicapped people don't curse and talk shit. I always think if someone's handicapped, then they're automatically some innocent angel. That's totally ridiculous of course, but I still thought it.

And nobody could get mad at him, because he's handicapped. Who's gonna yell at a handicapped dude with a stroke face and little dead baby arm, just because he cursed?

I liked Roscoe, and we had fun—but Roscoe was into me, too. I mean, *really* into me, and not subtle at all. Every day when he saw me, he'd come up to me and say:

Roscoe: "TIFF-A-KNEEEEE! You so booty-full! You look soooo good too-day!"

He would notice everything. I could change one little thing, and he would notice it. I'd come into work, he'd see me, his eyes would go all bugged out and crazy, and he'd slur out:

Roscoe: "Whooooaaaa, Tiff-a-Knee, you look soooo hot. I love your blue eye-shad-ooow."

He started bringing me Filet-O-Fish sandwiches on Fridays, because he learned that I liked them. When he saw I appreciated it, he started bringing me flowers on Mondays.

Roscoe: "Deese are for youuu, Tiff-a-Knee, for youuu house."

I could not put these flowers in my house. These were not regular flowers you buy at the store. I am pretty sure Roscoe stole them out of somebody's yard, because they had dirt and ants and bugs all over them. They were pretty, though.

Once he got to know me, Roscoe started asking me out on dates at least once a week.

Roscoe: "TIFF-A-KNEEEEE! You so booty-full. Can we go on
a date two-mar-oooow? You want to go on a date with meee?"

I would tell him that I had a man, and he would look sad. Then a few days later, he'd ask me out again, and we'd go through the same conversation. He was never pushy about it, always polite and respectful, but man—he *never* gave up.

One day, he asked me:

Roscoe: "What yer fay-vor-it cologne, Tiff-a-Knee? What youuu want your man to smell like?"

Tiffany: "Clean, Roscoe. I want him to smell clean."

Roscoe: "You like Old Spice? You like Brut? You like Cool Water? Cool Water smells clean?"

Tiffany: "I don't know if I like that, I don't even know what that stuff smells like. As long as he smells clean. I like my man to smell clean. My boyfriend's cologne is pretty good."

At the time, I was dating Titus, and he worked in the airport. In fact, he was part of the same department that Roscoe worked for, but for a different airline. I told Roscoe this, and he said:

Roscoe: "Okay, I go see yer boy-fren. I goin' smell him, I goin' find out what'chu like."

I didn't think about that weird-ass statement until about two months later, when I was going through the breakup with Titus. He had lost his job at the airport, and we were having serious problems, and Roscoe came up to me and said:

Roscoe: "Tiff-a-Knee, why youuu got a damn man who don't havva job? Youuu too good for dat, Tiff-a-Knee, your man gotta havva job!"

I don't know how Roscoe knew that, because I didn't tell nobody that my man got fired.

I wondered for a second if Roscoe had something to do with it, but that's ridiculous—how's a handicapped guy with a little baby arm gonna get my man fired?

The breakup with Titus was hard. I spent months getting over him, crying, being sad and fucked up.

Every day, Roscoe was telling me I'm beautiful. Even on the days I was coming in tired and burnt out, with nasty, puffy eyes, because I'd been crying all night, he still told me I'm beautiful.

Roscoe: "TIFF-A-KNEE! Youu are so booty-full! You look soooo good too-day!"

Roscoe gave me my space when I needed it, but he pretty quickly got back to asking me out. And now it went from once a week, to every single day.

Roscoe: "TIFF-A-KNEE! Youu are so booty-full! Can we go on a date? You want to go on a date with meee?"

One day, I was finally over my ex-boyfriend. I don't know what possessed me, maybe it was the Filet-O-Fish that Roscoe had just brought me, but I said:

Tiffany: "Yeah, fuck it. Let's go on a date, Roscoe. Let's do it."

His eyes bugged out, and his sideways mouth hung open. For a second, I thought maybe he was having a stroke. But then he snapped out of it:

Roscoe: "Fer reaaal? Fer reaaal, Tiff-a-Knee?"

Tiffany: "Yeah Roscoe, let's go out."

Roscoe: "Okay, oh my God, okay, aww right. Dis gonna be great, Tiff-a-Knee! We're gonna go to Hermosa Beach, to da Hennessey's, it's gonna be the best date evaaaa! We'll catch da 217 bus, den get the crosstown, then—"

Tiffany: "Roscoe, I got my own car, I'll pick you up."

He gave me his address and then ran out of work. I don't even think it was the end of his shift, he was just so excited that he bolted out of the airport.

The next evening, I pulled up to his place. I was thinking, *This is a pretty big house, considering he's handicapped and works as a baggage handler. How is he affording this? Does he live with his parents?*

Nope. Turns out it's one of those group homes for adults with disabilities. And I am here to straight pick up this man to go on a date. At a group home.

A girl answered the door. Clearly she had Down syndrome. She took one look at me and screamed at the top of her lungs:

"YOU MUSS BE TIFF-A-KNEEEE!!! YOU MUSS BE TIFF-A-KNEEEE!!! YOU ARE SOOO BOOTY-FULL! YOU ARE SOOO BOOTY-FULL!"

She started running in circles in the living room, throwing her hands in the air and screaming as loud as she could:

"EVERYONE COME SEE! TIFF-A-KNEE HERE, SHE IS SO BOOTY-FULL!! [deep breath] TIFF-A-KNEE HERE, SHE IS SO BOOTY-FULL!! [deep breath] EVERYONE COME SEE! TIFF-A-KNEE HERE, SHE IS SO BOOTY-FULL!!"

All I could think to myself is, *I gotta come over here every day. This is wonderful. This is how people should greet people. This is what I'm talkin' 'bout.*

As she was running in circles, screaming at the top of her lungs, the living room filled up with all sorts of different handicapped people. It was like—I don't even know how to describe it. Like, in that Rudolph Christmas special, the Island of Misfit Toys.

There was a dude in a wheelchair, who had this goofy smile that did not change one bit the whole time I was there. There was an older lady in there, she had Down syndrome, she was smiling and clapping. There was a young kid with his hands over his ears rocking back and forth on the sofa, but he was smiling, too. Roscoe came down the stairs, and he looked a little annoyed:

Roscoe: "Ever-buddy calm down, she my date, dis is my date, guys! Relax, okay! Relax, I see you guys lay-tah."

Roscoe was the alpha dog in the group home!

He was like the older brother trying to deal with his little brothers and sisters. They all hugged him and lined up at the door to say goodbye. Roscoe finally got through his people and to me, and he gave me flowers.

And yes, there were bugs in them.

Roscoe: "Tiff-a-Knee, I gonna show youuu sucha good time, we gunna have so much fuuuuun. We gunna eat da best buuurgers . . ."

On and on like that, the whole car ride. He finally calmed down by the time we got to Hermosa Beach, to a bar called Hennessey's. It was karaoke night.

I don't know if you've ever been to Hennessey's in Hermosa Beach, but this is a beachy, preppy, white-people bar. It's where the bros drink their brews, and the surfers sip their hurricanes, and they all just *white* together.

We were the ONLY black people in there. Even the busboys were white.

We ordered our drinks, and before they even came, Roscoe ran up to the stage. With his good arm, he grabbed the mic from the last person who sang. I am pretty sure there was a long line of people waiting their turns, but you know how polite these beachy white people are. They ain't gonna say nothing when someone like Roscoe grabs the mic.

He composed himself onstage as the DJ loaded the song. He waited patiently and anxiously for his song to start, hopping around just a little, like a kid that had to pee.

Then it started. And he started singing. He was not just doing regular karaoke. This dude was straight belting him some Luther Vandross. I mean, he was *into* it.

"A chair is still a chair,
Even if no one is sitting there . . ."

Now understand, Roscoe was handicapped, so I'll be nice about it: his singing was terrible. He was off-key and tone-deaf. It was just bad, horrible singing.

But he knew all the words, and he knew all of Luther's moves, and he put his heart into it. He had on his little burgundy blazer, and he was swinging his little dead baby arm around, all suave and shit.

But yeah, it sounded just horrible.

This is the part I remember the most, not just because of Roscoe's horrible singing, but because of this white lady sitting in front of me. She kept looking back at me. I was drinking my wine and trying to enjoy the fact that my handicapped date was singing his heart out, but this white lady would not stop looking at me. Finally she turned around, looked me up and down, and said, "You are so strong."

For real—she turned her whole chair around, and said—I am fucking quoting her, "You are so strong."

I wanted to curl up under the table and die.

When Roscoe finished singing, everybody went nuts and cheered and screamed and clapped. You know how white people do, they just encourage and cheer anybody who lets it all hang out and just don't give a fuck. Roscoe got excited by all this attention and sang another quick song. I can't even remember what it was, I was still so mad and embarrassed about that comment from that bitch.

He finally came and sat down. He was sweating and all out of breath, because he basically just performed a concert. He took a long swig of his beer, reached over the table with his good arm, grabbed my hand with that strong hand, while his little dead hand rested on the table. He looked all deep into my eyes, and I was looking at him, and all I could think was that I wanted to kill the rest of my wine. I wanted to down the rest of it, but I didn't want to seem like a lush. He was looking at me, and he said:

Roscoe: "Tiff-a-Knee, I juss wanna tell youuuu, I feel like I'm da luckiest man alive. If I die to-mar-oooow, it'd be my happiess day of my life. I'm serious, if I die to-mar-oooow, dat's fine, dis da most wunnerful day. A girl as booty-full as youu to be out wiffa guy like me, is the most wunnerful day evaa of my life."

Tiffany: "Oh, Roscoe, it's no problem, we work together, we cool."

Roscoe: "No, Tiff-a-Knee, you don't unnerstan. Dis the most special day evaa. I want it to be magical for us."

He started crying. Like, big-ass man tears coming out of his eyes. And then snot starts coming out of his nose. He just turned into a hot mess, as he told me I was so special and how amazing this day was for him. He took a minute to compose himself and said:

Roscoe: "I could die, it's okay, I'm okay if I die now. Dat's how special dis is to me, Tiff-a-Knee."

Here I was, sitting in a crowded bar, with a man crying, snot coming out of his nose, and honestly, all I could think was one thing: *I'm going to fuck the shit outta Roscoe.*

For real. That's what I kept saying to myself, *"I am going to fuck the shit outta Roscoe."*

First off, I'd never seen a man cry for me. I'd never seen a man express his love for me like this. Nothing like this had ever happened to me ever before.

I just thought to myself, *Well, this is who I'm supposed to be with, obviously. This is who I'm supposed to spend my time with, this man who loves me so much and does so much for me and adores me like this. That's right. I'm going to fuck him. I'm gonna fuck the shit out of Roscoe tonight.*

I didn't care about nothing else. Fuck that judgmental white lady. I downed my wine, we got another round, and then we went back to my place.

My date movie at the time was *The Wiz*. If I liked you, and I put on *The Wiz*, that was a good sign. And if you could sit and watch *The Wiz* through the Scarecrow part, I'm fucking. If you can sit through Michael Jackson's scene, that's it, it's on.

Well, Roscoe did not sit through *The Wiz*. That's because he was acting the whole thing out. HE KNEW ALL THE WORDS!

You know how white people do with *The Rocky Horror Picture Show*? Just like that.

> *Roscoe:* "Come on, Tiff-a-Knee, come dance wiff me! Ease on down, ease on down da rooooaaaad!"

Oh my God, did he love this movie. It was like I dropped into some musical theater summer camp in my own house.

But you know what? I love that movie, too! Fuck it, I got up and danced and sang *The Wiz* with him.

By the time it got to the Lena Horne part, the end of the movie, it was time for business. I leaned in and gave him a little kiss on his cheek. He said:

> *Roscoe:* "Ohhh Tiff-a-Knee, youu don't wanna do dat, don't do dat, Tiff-a-Knee. You don't know what'chu gettin' yursef into."

I leaned in, gave him another kiss. He got all serious:

> *Roscoe:* "Okay, Tiff-a-Knee, I seer-ee-us. I warned you and I not gunna warn you no more. Don't do that, okay, you

don't know what you're doing. I'm seer-ee-us, very seer-ee-us, Tiff-a-Knee."

He smelled real good. Whatever it was, it was good, and it was kinda getting me horny.

I did not realize it at the time, but thinking back on it, I am pretty sure he was wearing the same cologne that Titus used to wear. He must have actually went and smelled that motherfucker, now that I think about it.

He did smell good, though. Except his breath smelled like corn chips, but that was normal for Roscoe.

"Whatever, Roscoe, you smell all good and stuff," I said and leaned in again to give him another kiss.

He wasn't kidding with that warning. Roscoe took that third kiss as his cue, and he straight went to work. He grabbed my face with that strong hand, and he started tonguing me down. Next thing I knew, all my clothes were off, he was stroking my face with his strong hand, still kissing me, while he's putting on a condom with that little hand.

I was like, *Oh shit! This motherfucker's a professional fucker.* Here I was, all proud of myself, thinking I was fixing to be his first. Yeah, I was fixing to blow his mind, but hell no! He's been fucking all kinds of handicapped bitches or something, nurses or whoever, because ain't no virgin on Earth have skills like this.

He finally got his T. rex arm to put the condom on, and he moved in. And yes, I know what you're going to ask:

He had dick for days.

And for real . . . he tore it up.

He straight tore up the pussy. His dick game was off the chain!

He took control and laid me back and went to work, and it felt amazing. I was on my back in missionary, enjoying the hell out of this fuck. My pussy was feeling so good.

And then I opened my eyes.

Oh hell. I'm looking at him, and it's like—his face is just twisted as fuck. It was so contorted and screwed up, it was horrifying to look at. You know when someone is concentrating, they make funny faces? Yeah, well, it was like a Halloween mask was doing that.

I closed my eyes in fright, but damn, it would start feeling really good down there, and then I would open my eyes again, and be like *"Oh, no."* It was like a scary movie, except that my pussy felt great.

The thing that really messed me up was that he was holding himself up with that good arm, and his dead little baby hand was dangling over my face. And you know, it's Roscoe, so he's sweating and drooling and shit, and it's dripping on my forehead.

The sweat and the drool, it was too nasty. I had to do something, but I didn't want the sex to stop.

Tiffany: "Roscoe, hit this from the back."

Roscoe: "Ohhhh, youuuu want me to tap dat azz from da back! YOU AIN'T GOTTA AXE ME TWICE!"

He took his strong arm, slid it underneath me, grabbed my opposite hip, and in one motion, flipped me over. I landed right on my hands and knees instantly. I don't even know how he did it. It was some Cirque du Soleil shit.

He was right in me, holding my waist with that good hand, smacking my ass with that little dead hand, and he was just fucking my pussy up. I could kind of feel him drooling, but I didn't give a shit. As long as I didn't have to see his Halloween sex faces, it was cool, because his dick was amazing.

He was saying all the normal things guys say during sex, then all of a sudden, the craziest fucking thing happened.

Roscoe: "Damn girl, you got some good pussy."

His voice turned normal.

He went from his mush-mouth, long-ass vowel words you could barely understand, to talking like a normal man. And with a deep, sexy-ass Billy Dee Williams voice.

Roscoe: "Yeah Tiffany, you like this dick, don't you, sexy girl?"

Hell yeah, I do!

I started feeling like, *Okay, I must have magical powers, I can heal people with my pussy.*

He kept talking normal, and then he came hard, and plopped down next to me. The sex had been amazing, but I was even more excited that I healed this motherfucker with my pussy! I got a magical unicorn pussy!

I got all sweet and turned to him.

Tiffany: "Roscoe, you were so good, you want something to drink, baby?"

Roscoe: "Yeah, baby, I'd love something to drink."

I walked to the kitchen, and for real in my twenty-two-year-old brain, I honestly thought to myself, *I fucking healed this guy. I made him healthy. This is the greatest ghetto fairy tale ever.*

I poured him a nice, cold glass of water, and I stopped in the bathroom to fix my hair and look good for my newly healed man.

Tiffany: "Here you go, baby, here's your water."

Roscoe: "Tank youuu, Tiff-a-Knee."

Oh, hell no! It wore off!

My magical pussy power is only temporary!

I was seriously depressed. I honestly thought for a second my pussy had powers and that I turned this incredibly sweet handicapped man into a normal boyfriend (except for that one arm, but still). Yes, I know that's fucking nonsense, but I thought it.

Oh, well. He may not be healed, but handicapped or not, he can still fuck.

I was off work the next day and the day after that, so I made him call in to work sick, and I kept him at my place that whole time. We was fucking for two days straight. Sometimes sleeping and eating, but mainly fucking.

I did most of the cooking, but to his credit, he made sandwiches for us. But I didn't go in there and watch him make them, because I didn't want to see that dead baby hand on my food. I kept that image out of my mind.

Eventually, I took him back to his place, and I kept thinking this thought:

How can I take him around my friends?

On the one hand, I think I love this dude. He's an amazing human and the best sex I've ever had—just so loving and caring. He was the shit to me, the awesomest in the world.

At the same time, he's handicapped. There ain't no way around that fact. I can't take him around my friends. I can hear their voices in my head:

"You dating a handicapped guy who rides the bus? Is you serious? You getting community service for this? Did your probation officer tell you this counts or something?"

"Tiffany, you were an extra in an Xzibit video! Why are you messing with this guy? You could be fucking Xzibit! What's wrong with you, Tiffany?"

"He can't keep his drool in his mouth! He only got one arm that works! Bitch, what are you doing?"

Over and over it went, in my mind. There was no escaping the fact that I cannot date a handicapped guy.

I got to work the next day, and Roscoe was there. We'd had zero discussion of how we'd act at work. He was super-excited to see me and everything, and I mean super-excited. As he walked up, I could see his dick getting hard in his pants.

Tiffany: "Yo Roscoe, we gotta talk at lunch. We need to have a conversation."

Roscoe: "Oh yeaaaa, we gunna talk awww right!"

He grabbed his dick and smiled at me.

Tiffany: "Don't do that, Roscoe. A real talk. A conversation."

Roscoe: "I know a place we can havva talk awwright. A goooood talk."

Tiffany: "No, we're going to meet in the Center Air, it's a restaurant in the center of the airport. Meet me in the Center Air where everybody be at, we'll meet right there."

Lunch came around, and we met there and started talking. Roscoe was happy and serene and had no idea what was coming. I felt so bad.

Roscoe: "Tiff-a-Knee, youuu so booty-full to-day. I was thinking bout'chu all night lass night—"

Tiffany: "Roscoe, shh. Stop. We have to talk."

I took a deep breath and launched in.

I told him I was shallow. I told him I was insecure. I kept talking about what a bad girlfriend I was, and how I wasn't ready for a relationship. I said I knew he wanted me to be his girlfriend, but that maybe it would work in our next lifetime. I hit him with the Erykah Badu; maybe next lifetime we can have a better life. But I'm too immature right now. I probably rambled for twenty minutes, before he got it and stopped me:

Roscoe: "Are youu sayin' youu can't date meee?"

Tiffany: "Yes Roscoe, that is what I am saying."

Roscoe: "What? Are you fuckin' seer-ee-us? Are youu sayin' youu don't wanna be wiff me?"

Tiffany: "Not like that, Roscoe, I want to be your friend, I just can't be your woman. I can't be in a serious relationship with you. I don't know how I can handle that."

Roscoe: "Arrr youu sayin' youu can't be my gurl?"

Tiffany: "Yes Roscoe, that's what I'm saying."

He looked at me, and his face nearly broke my heart. It was the rawest look of pain and heartbreak I have ever seen on any face, ever in my life.

Roscoe: "Okay."

I almost started crying, and I was so close to grabbing his hand and taking it all back, when he stood up.

Roscoe: "Well . . . FUCK YOU THEN! DATS WHY YER PUSSY GARBAGE!"

Tiffany: "WHAT???"

Roscoe: "YER PUSSY IS GARBAGE."

Roscoe stormed off. I was in motherfucking shock. I wanted to yell something back at him, but there were people everywhere. And besides, what am I going to yell back? "Well you're fucking handi-capped!" or "My pussy IS NOT garbage!"?

I didn't know what to say or do. I just sat there in shock, until my break was over. Then I went back to my counter.

When I got back to the ticket counter, he didn't even want to throw my bags no more. He went down to the other end of the counter and threw somebody else's bags. And he gave me the evil eye the rest of the day.

Then, I didn't see him after that for a few days. I went to his bosses at work. They said, "We don't know where Roscoe is, Roscoe just stopped coming to work."

After a few weeks, I thought to myself, *Damn, maybe I shouldn't have broke up with him. Maybe that was my blessing from God. If he was my blessing and I shitted on my blessing, that's not cool. I need to find him and talk to him.*

I went back to the address where I'd picked him up for our date. The same girl with Down syndrome answered the door. She said Roscoe was gone.

"Roscoe left, Roscoe not here no more, but you still so booty-full, you so booty-full!"

Nobody at his group home knew where he went. I even talked to the lady that ran the place. She said she didn't know where he moved to or where he went. He left without even telling them where he was going.

I didn't know where else to look for him, or what else to do. He was gone. He just vanished.

Nobody knew what happened to Roscoe.

I didn't tell anyone about Roscoe and me. I just kept it to myself.

I still have all these what if's go through my mind. I seriously think to myself, *What if he was an angel from heaven? What if God was testing me to see if I can have compassion and overlook people's physical handicaps and look at the beauty of their souls?* Roscoe was such a beautiful person, he had a truly beautiful soul.

He was always so positive and supportive. Whatever I said I wanted to do, everyone else put me down or told me I couldn't do it. Not Roscoe. He would always encourage me. He was one of the first people I told when I decided to start doing comedy.

Tiffany: "I'm about to go full-time in comedy, Roscoe."

Roscoe: "TIFF-A-KNEE! Youu do soo good! Youu soo fun-neeee! Tell me when youu doin' it, I'm going to come see youuu."

Tiffany: "I'm doing open mics right now, maybe when my shows get bigger, then you can come to the show."

Roscoe: "Oh, you're so fun-nee, youu make everybody laugh, you're going to be the best comedian, you're going to be the best."

He would always be so encouraging. Even though life had dealt him such a bad hand, he was just a positive motherfucker.

And then he was gone, and it was my fault.

For years, I didn't tell none of my friends about him. Then

I ran into one of my old coworkers, and I told her. She about choked:

> *Friend:* "You fucked Roscoe? Oh my God. How did you end up fucking Roscoe? I remember he used to talk about you every day, and if you didn't show up to work, he'd be wondering where you were, so worried about you. How did you end up fucking Roscoe?"

I told her what happened, the whole story. Then she got all mad at me:

> *Friend:* "You never told no one that? If you don't talk about that onstage, you wrong! You have to go talk about that, because handicapped people need love—they need love too, they people."

> *Tiffany:* "Yeah, I know. I know I'm going to heaven, too. Roscoe taught me that."

> *Friend:* "What do you mean you know you're going to heaven?"

> *Tiffany:* "Because I fucked Roscoe. Roscoe is probably an angel, a fallen angel. I feel like Roscoe was like the John Travolta character in the movie *Michael*. He came to earth to teach me to be humble and that all people need love no matter who or what they are. Because I fucked him, that's why he disappeared. That's why we don't see him no more,

because he went back to heaven. Only a heavenly dick could fuck me the way Roscoe did."

She kinda paused, and then we both broke out laughing. She told me:

Friend: "Well . . . I don't know about all *that*. But still, you gotta talk about this. You gotta tell the world about your handicapped angel."

In my heart, I knew she was right: I couldn't keep it to myself.

How I Got
(Restarted) in Comedy

I quit comedy when I was eighteen, so I could get a job and provide for myself.

I got restarted in comedy at twenty-two, because I had to stomp a bitch for disrespecting me.

It was Bertha. Yes, that same Bertha, the stripper that Titus the Boyfriend couldn't pimp, but I could. Here's how it all went down.

When I was still pimping her, Bertha asked me if I could pick her up from the strip club one day. She had me take her to a party. When we arrived, Titus the Boyfriend was there.

Tiffany: "I don't know if I should stay for this."

Titus: "Nah, it's cool, Tiff. It's cool. I ain't tripping. I get it. Let bygones be bygones. Me and Bertha, we in a relationship now."

Tiffany: "Okay. Cool."

I pulled Bertha aside and told her:

Tiffany: "I will always be cool with you. Just don't ever disrespect me. If you ever disrespect me, it's going to be a motherfucking problem."

That night was fine. I was drinking 211 beer. Now, I don't know if you ever heard of this beer, but it's 99 cents. This is the shit that bums buy to get all fucked up on the cheap. It makes you fucking crazy. Of course, Titus the Po' Pimp has this at his party.

I drank some and fell asleep on the couch. When I woke up, it was late. Titus and Bertha were on the floor, right next to the couch I was sleeping on. Fucking. Like, right next to me. I jumped up:

Tiffany: "BITCH, WHAT I TELL YOU ABOUT DISRESPECTING ME?"

I just started stomping on her. I was straight ghetto-stomping her out. She curled into a ball and started crying.

Tiffany: "GET YOUR MOTHERFUCKING ASS UP, BITCH! I'M FIXIN' TO BEAT YO ASS SOME MO!"

Bertha: "Stop! I'm not going to fight you, Tiffany. I'm not going to fight you. I'm going to call the police!"

Tiffany: "CALL THE MOTHERFUCKING POLICE! I'll just get your ass deported up out this bitch. You fixing to get deported right back to Jamaica, bitch! I know you here illegally, I'm the one fucking pimping you!! What's up now??"

Titus tried to stop me from stomping on her. I did what any black woman who was being disrespected would do: I straight punched him in the mouth.

Tiffany: "DON'T YOU TOUCH ME, NIGGA! I WILL KILL YOU!"

Titus: "Why you tripping???"

I just started going berserk. I was drunk as hell on 211, screaming at the top of my lungs, Bertha was crying, Titus was screaming, I was throwing furniture—it was for-real black woman craziness.

Then his homeboy picked me up from behind and carried me out the house to my car.

Needless to say, I stopped talking to Bertha after that. I had no more words for her. That's how I stopped pimping her.

Maybe two months later, Titus showed up to my house with a ring, asking would I marry him. He had put rose petals all over my car in the shape of a heart and a bunch more all over my yard.

Tiffany: "Are you fucking serious right now?"

Titus: "Tiffany, you the smartest woman I know. Please, will you marry me?"

Oh, yeah—the ring still had the price tag on it, from Kmart. It was $38.

A $38 ring. That's what he thought I was worth.

Tiffany: "Get the fuck out of here with this cheap-ass ring. Fuck you, don't ever talk to me again."

I was so pissed. I cussed him out. I was angry all night.

The next day, I was so disturbed emotionally, I started crying. I cried all day, all night. I could not stop crying at work.

Then I started to bleed. At first I thought it was just my period, but it wouldn't stop. It was heavy. I was feeling weak.

This went on for weeks. I was bleeding so much, I eventually went through every maxi-pad in all of LAX. I seriously think I used every one of them huge free maxis in all the women's bathrooms in the whole damn airport.

Eventually, it just ran down my leg. It was just like I had peed on myself, but it was blood pouring out of me.

My manager at the airlines was the same nice, nerdy white guy I talked about before.

Manager: "Tiffany, that's blood. You're bleeding. You're standing in a puddle of blood. You have to go. We're calling 911. Are you pregnant or something?"

Tiffany: "No, I'm not pregnant or anything. I can't stop bleeding. I don't know why I'm bleeding."

It was so embarrassing. All I could think about was that I didn't have insurance, and I couldn't pay for an ambulance.

Tiffany: "I don't want to pay for an ambulance. Just call my grandma."

My grandma came and took me to the hospital. They couldn't figure out what was wrong. There was nothing in my tests. They kept me in the hospital overnight. Nothing showed up that was actually wrong. No fibroids. Nothing. They couldn't figure it out.

They gave me some medication, like some birth control stuff that's supposed to make it stop. My stomach also felt like it was on fire, like it was burning up. They said I didn't have ulcers or nothing like that, but they gave me something for it.

I got so skinny. I was down to 110 pounds.

I felt like I was dying. I was crying all the time, bleeding all the time. My stomach was hurting all the time. I was so fucking sick.

They eventually gave me some antidepressants. They recommended that I see a psychiatrist, so I did.

The therapist was nice. She talked to me all about my life and everything, and I was constantly crying in there. But it was weird, because everything I said, she would laugh. She'd be giggling and stuff.

Tiffany: "Why you laughing? This shit's not funny! My life fucking sucks!"

She'd stop and compose herself. But pretty soon, she'd be laughing again.

Therapist: "Tiffany, what do you love to do? What makes you happy?"

Tiffany: "I like teeth. Maybe I should just be a dentist, because I really love teeth. I really like the way teeth look, but I don't want to hurt anybody, so maybe I could just be the dental assistant."

She laughed at that, too.

Therapist: "Have you ever thought about comedy?"

Tiffany: "It's funny you say that. I like seeing people smile, hearing laughter. That makes me happy. You know, I used to do comedy, in high school."

Remember when I went to Laugh Factory Comedy Camp? And how great that was? And remember how I had stopped doing comedy when I had got kicked out of my grandma's house at eighteen? I stopped doing comedy because it wasn't paying anything. Right? I told her all about that. About how great it was for me, and why I quit.

Therapist: "Well, maybe you should start doing that again, at least as a hobby. Do stand-up comedy again. It made you so happy then, why not now?"

Well, fuck. I forgot about that. I forgot how much I loved comedy. I forgot how much joy it brought me.

I decided to try it, do some open mics. Basically, open mic is some shit that anyone can get up and do.

I thought about it, and I prepared, and I got ready. I got up and did five minutes, and I got a ton of laughs. It was amazing. I went back the next night, did the same five-minute set, but with some improvements. It was even better. People loved it.

Now, don't get me wrong, it's not like I was bringing the house down and people were in tears at my brilliance, throwing roses on the stage, and screaming my name. That shit didn't happen for at least ten more years ☺

But open mics are tough. Most of the people suck and aren't funny, and the crowd can get annoyed and become hostile. To get any laughs at an open mic is really good. And I got laughs. People liked me. They enjoyed it.

It was like, the smallest thing, but it was so profound for me. I had known this at fifteen, that this was my calling, and I had quit. And now here I was, telling my stories and hearing people laugh at them and feeling that rush again.

I started doing lots of open mics, getting my comedy chops back again. And the more time that I spent on comedy, the more the bleeding stopped. The stomach pains stopped. The crying and depression stopped.

I don't know how or why, but all the bad shit stopped. All of it. Just from doing open mics.

I started to become more happy and more joyous. I started thinking more positive. I started reading positive books.

Then Titus tried to get me back. He started coming to my open mics, and he would write jokes and put them in my mailbox or whatever. They were terrible jokes! Fucking knock-knock shit! I was done with him, though. I'd already fucked Roscoe by this point, and I had re-found comedy, I didn't have no time in my life for a fake pimp who thought I was worth $38.

I kept doing open mics and kept feeling better, and then I got my first paid gig. It almost derailed me, and sent me off comedy forever.

One of my aunties called me and said her friend was having

some women's group meeting or something, and they wanted me to perform at their event.

Aunt: "And it pays $50."

Tiffany: "Yeah, right. How much time they want me to do? Two hours?"

Aunt: "They want you to do fifteen minutes. That's it."

Tiffany: "Oh hell yes!"

I got there, and I knew it was a women's event ahead of time, but damn, there were NO men there. I had come with another co-median friend, a guy, and he was like:

Friend: "Tiffany, a lot of these ladies sure is leaning in close to each other."

Tiffany: "Oh, they probably can't hear each other over the music."

I came out onto the stage, all excited and ready to give my fifteen-minute set. I'd been practicing and refining it at open mics. My jokes were all about dating and having a man, and this woman yelled out:

Woman: "I bet you I can fuck you better than your man!"

I was like, *What did she say?* I just stood there confused for a second, because I just did not believe she could have said that. Then I kept going with another joke about a man. Then some other woman yelled out:

Woman: "We don't want to hear about no men. Damn, baby. Your body look good. You fine! Let's talk about that!"

I'd been interrupted twice now, and I was too confused to keep going, so I blurted out, kind of kidding:

Tiffany: "What is this? A lesbian event or some shit?"

Everybody in unison was like, "Yeah."

Tiffany: "Oh, shit! Nobody told me this shit!"

That got a big laugh. I was so uncomfortable. I didn't know what to do, so I just did what I always do when I'm uncomfortable: I made shit WAY WORSE.

I started talking about dick even more, and then I just kept talking about dick. I was going on about all the dicks, and then some woman blurts out:

Lesbian: "I got a drawer full of dicks for you, and you can pick any one you want, baby!"

That got the best laugh yet from the crowd.

Tiffany: "Okay, no. I was talking about one that is actually attached to a man. I love men. Let me tell you about men and they dicks!"

I just went into this whole thing about how awesome men are, and how much I love men, which was pretty ironic, considering that the best man I had ever been with in my life lived in a group home for the handicapped.

If I had been a more experienced comedian, I would have talked about that and made a ton of jokes about that, and the crowd would have loved it. But I wasn't there yet. I was just being antagonizing and awkward.

Lesbian: "We don't want no dick lovers here!"

I just started laughing at that, mainly because nobody else was laughing, and I was that uncomfortable. They were only laughing when somebody was heckling me, and I was so nervous.

Lesbian: "Get your funky ass off the stage, dick lover."

Tiffany: "Oh hell no! See, you can heckle me if you want, but don't be trying to get me off stage. I'mma stay up here my whole time, and I'mma get ALL my money."

I did that. I stayed on the full fifteen minutes.

When I got off the stage, I felt like a piece of meat. If you think only men can make a woman feel horrible, you don't know shit about other women. I felt about the worst I had felt in a long time. And the dude I was with, he was no help:

Friend: "Yeah, I don't know about this. If you get reactions like this all the time, I don't think you should do comedy."

I was pretty depressed. I was reconsidering whether this was for me.

Then the promoter handed me fifty bucks.

I just tanked onstage, the worst I have EVER tanked in my comedy life, and I got $50?!?!

This was great!

I knew right then, in the middle of all those lesbians offering me their dildos, that I was gonna do this for the rest of my life.

I've thought about that moment a lot, and why I felt like that. How could such a painful, embarrassing moment become the turning point in my life?

When I think about it, I had already made the decision to be a comedian earlier in my life. When I rode that damn bus all day, two days in a row, just to stand in the courtroom, as a fifteen-year-old foster kid that nobody loved. I told the judge that I was gonna be a successful comedian. That was the day I decided in my heart to be a comedian and make people laugh.

But what happened on the Lesbian Bomb Night was that when I did that show, and those women heckled me, and they were laughing at each other's heckles—people were still laughing. Yeah, the laughing was at my expense, but people laughed, *and* I was paid.

I got $50 for fifteen minutes. If I could string together, like, even just four fifteen-minute segments per day, I could be making bank!

But it wasn't just about making money. When I'm onstage, I feel like it's—it's where I am supposed to be. It's who I am. When I am onstage, it's like this adrenaline rush. You gotta show up and be on and bust your ass, or people will not laugh. And nothing else makes my mind work so fast and so hard. I like that feeling.

Getting paid that night allowed me to imagine a place for myself in the universe doing something I loved.

It's a risk though. Everything you get on that stage is earned, not given. You don't know anybody in the room, and you don't know what these people are gonna laugh at, if they're gonna like it or not. It's very scary.

But the weird flip side of this is that I know I'm safe up there. I know they can say whatever they want to, but nobody's gonna hurt me up there. If somebody does hurt me, it's gonna be in a room full of witnesses. I just feel the safest there. And even if I bomb and they say terrible things about me, people will laugh at me, and I'll get paid anyway. In the worst case, I get paid to make people laugh!

And the power that comes with it is intoxicating. It's better than any drug. As soon as I step my foot out on that stage, all these eyes are on me. I feel like I'm the bravest and safest person in the room. Everybody's anticipating what I have to say, and I have this power that I don't have anywhere else. Sometimes it works, sometimes it doesn't, but it feels so fucking good.

And then, when I come off the stage, I've got this high. Even when I do bad, I get that high. And then the high starts to come down, but once they hand me my money, then I'm back high again. Whether it was a good experience or a bad experience, I was compensated for it.

That's validation.

I felt all of this then in a flash—at that moment the guy gave me $50 for doing fifteen minutes of terrible comedy. I knew, at the core of my being, that my job was going to be to get onstage and make people laugh, and get paid for it.

Dating

Dating has been hard for me my whole life, and almost none of the relationships I've had have worked out that well. I guess that's obvious, since I'm still single, as of the writing of this book.

How Comedy Fucks with Relationships

I talk about Roscoe onstage sometimes. That shit does *not* go over well with some guys. My last boyfriend first heard about Roscoe during a set of mine:

Ex-Boyfriend: "How long did it take you to write that joke?"

Tiffany: "No time at all. I lived that joke."

Ex-Boyfriend: "You lying, that can't be true."

Tiffany: "Oh no—Roscoe is real. That whole story is true."

Ex-Boyfriend: "FOR REAL? You for real fucked a handicapped dude? I know you got a big heart and everything but GODDAM, Tiffany!"

Tiffany: "So what, it happened years ago."

Ex-Boyfriend: "You said it was the best sex you ever had! Now I gotta compete with a handicapped dude? What I got to do to be better than him?"

Tiffany: "It's not about that. It was the passion, the intensity of it all."

Ex-Boyfriend: "What exactly do you want, do you want me to make my hand like a little dinosaur hand to smack you with my fingertips? Is that what you want? Make funny noises when we fuck? You want me to drool?"

Tiffany: "No, it was Roscoe, it was different, you're different. You don't have to be angry—you're better than Roscoe in other ways."

That was the wrong thing to say. He went crazy over that shit. Angry, yelling about how much better he was than some handicapped dude who lived in a group home. Shit, I would hope so! If you gotta point that out, you already in trouble.

Later on we were at a store together, and there was a dude working, you could tell he was touched. He was smiling all big and got wide eyes and he came up to us all fast:

Touched Worker: "Y'all need help? I help you, I help you!!"

He was real nice and trying to be helpful, but my ex comes barging between us:

Ex-Boyfriend: "You stand back, Tiffany. Thank you sir, we're good. You can go away now."

Touched Worker: "OK cool, if you need help, you ask me!!"

That guy was so nice, and my ex was kind of mean to him.

Ex-Boyfriend: "I know you want to fuck that motherfucker, don't you Tiffany? I can tell by the way you're smiling at him. Stop smiling goddam it. I can't leave you nowhere. You wanna fuck this handicapped dude, I know you would."

Tiffany: "I might, I might."

I was kidding—obviously—but he got all angry again.

Ex-Boyfriend: "So you like that in a guy? If Tyson Beckford and a motherfucker missing an arm come in, who are you going to fuck? The motherfucker missing an arm, ain't you?"

Tiffany: "Stop tripping."

Ex-Boyfriend: "Stop tripping? I didn't fuck no handicapped. I gotta watch you now, I gotta be on the lookout for dudes with shit wrong, creepin' on my girl!"

A few weeks later, he was going through some old messages of mine on Instagram, still on this handicapped thing.

Ex-Boyfriend: "Look at this dude, saying he love you and

want to marry you! He look a little touched, look at his eye. Oh shit, you probably like him, I'mma block this motherfucker off your page."

Tiffany: "Why are you even in my shit like that, we've only been dating five months, it's not that serious. It's really not that serious."

Ex-Boyfriend: "I don't know, man, what if we get married, Tiffany? You're going to cheat on me with somebody with a disability?"

Tiffany: "I wouldn't cheat on you with nobody. If I wanted to cheat, I would just leave you."

Ex-Boyfriend: "YOU'D LEAVE ME FOR A DUDE WITH A DISABILITY!!?"

Tiffany: "No! Roscoe's the only handicapped dude I've been with, he's the only one. I don't have a variety of handicapped dudes."

Ex-Boyfriend: "Yeah right, Tiff, yeah right."

He did not believe me. He eventually got way back into my social media, and found a dude that I did used to mess with who got shot.

Ex-Boyfriend: "Look at this motherfucker, you told him you love him, and he in a wheelchair!"

Tiffany: "Well yeah, and that was three years ago. I did love him when we were dating."

Ex-Boyfriend: "This motherfucker in a wheelchair! I knew you liked handicapped!"

Tiffany: "When I was in love with him, when I was with him, he was not in a wheelchair. He got shot in the back, okay? That's why he's in a wheelchair."

Ex-Boyfriend: "I bet you were fucking in that wheelchair."

Tiffany: "Stop trippin'!"

Ex-Boyfriend: "I bet you would."

Anytime we had an argument, he would always bring up Roscoe or some kind of handicapped dick.

Well, we're not dating anymore. I guess that was easy to predict.

Other Guys I've Dated

I've dated a few policemen, and that was generally cool. Cops tend to be pretty good dudes. They are strong and polite, and they treat you right.

Well, not all of them. One of the guys, he ended up going to jail for robbing some Mexican fruit stands. He was a crooked cop.

I didn't know about him robbing the fruit stands, obviously, but I had a feeling something was off with him. When he would come to my house, he always put his gun on my dresser. It made me uncomfortable. It was like he was subconsciously saying, "Don't try nothing, bitch, or I'mma shoot you." That's what I felt. I didn't like that, so I backed off of him.

Good thing, too. I don't want to date no guy who robs poor Mexicans just trying to make some money selling fruit. That ain't right.

I dated two dope dealers, but there's nothing really funny about that. They're in jail, too. Come to think of it, I've dated about five guys who ended up in jail in some form.

One was this African dude who would always bring me clothes.

Well, I didn't really date him. It felt like I dated him, because he would call me so much, and he would bring me shoes and clothes that didn't fit. He put them in front of my house—like, right at the front door, like some sort of broke-ass Santa Claus.

I never went anywhere with him, because who leaves gifts at your door? And they were bad gifts, like really small clothes, double zero clothes. Or a pantsuit, and it's double zero, too. I don't wear a double zero. I'm not close to that size.

He brought me some Dada shoes, but they were a size six. I wear a ten. I was like, *ugh*. I didn't like that. I threw the clothes and the shoes away, and then he stopped bringing me things, because he went to jail.

He was running some of those Nigerian prince email scams. Using people's credit cards and checks, for identity theft. Hitting up old people for their money, that kind of stuff.

The Nice Guy

I dated a lawyer once. He was much older than me, like sixty, and he was so nice. He was always kind, always polite, and bought me nice things. He took me nice places, taught me a lot, was easy to talk to, a good communicator, and we had a lot of fun. Wherever we'd go, we would have a good time. We could go to a baby shower and still have fun, and we went to that kind of stuff all the time. He was dope.

But that's not why I dated him. To be honest, I dated him for racist reasons.

I dated him because he was white. At least, I thought he was. I didn't ask him, I just assumed.

I found out the truth when he went in for surgery on a torn rotator cuff. I went with him to the hospital to help him afterwards, because I'm a good girlfriend. When he was asleep, I wanted to see if we was healthy—you know, because we'd been hooking up without a condom for a while.

So I went through his charts, and right there, plain as day on his blood test, it said he's African-American. I went up to the nurse, all confused.

Tiffany: "He's not African-American. Why y'all got this on here? He came in here with me, I know him."

Nurse: "No, that's his chart. That's what it says."

I got sad, because I really thought I was dating a white man. When he woke up, I gently broached the subject:

Tiffany: "You black?!?!"

Old Boyfriend: "I don't normally talk about it."

He didn't know his mom. He was raised by his white, English father in London. When he asked his dad about his mom, his dad was like, "Your mom was mixed, but she was a harlot." Some English people call a ho a harlot, I guess. So his dad was calling his mom a ho.

You know the sad thing? If he'd been white, I might have kept dating him.

Well, maybe. There were other problems. He was also old.

He kept asking me to have babies with him. That didn't make sense. Here he was, sitting around with a messed up shoulder, already sixty, and he wants me to have a baby.

First off, he can't hold a baby with that shoulder!

Second, I'm not about to have to change your diaper and the baby's diaper. That's too much work.

Third, he already had two grown kids. What if they have babies? Now I'm getting grandpa dick. I don't want grandpa dick. I'm cool with baby daddy dick, but grandpa dick is no good.

That's how I felt, anyway. But he was the best boyfriend I ever had. If he was like twenty years younger, it would have been cool.

Toxic Shock

This isn't really a boyfriend story, but it kinda fits in this chapter, 'cause I wanted this doctor to be my boyfriend. Here's how it went down.

When I was thirteen—right before my mom hit that baby with a two-by-four and I got put in foster care—I got toxic shock syndrome.

I got toxic shock because I was using a super-absorbent tampon and I probably should have just been using a junior-sized tampon.

I didn't even know how to really use it right. I had the applicator in there and everything.

I went through the school day, I got home from school, and then I took the tampon out. I was itching and scratching all over. I just felt so sick. I was telling my mom, and my mom was like:

Mama: "She's just faking. She not sick. She's just faking."

Grandma: "She got a fever though, she got a fever."

Mama: "She all right. She going to be fine. Just take this Herbalife. That's what you need to do, just take this Herbalife."

To this day, I hate Herbalife because of this incident. She was making me swallow these pills, but soon as I swallowed them, I threw them up. Anything I drank—water, juice, whatever—I threw up.

Mama: "Oh, she acting. She acting. Stop acting like you sick. Stop acting like you got a problem. You just acting."

Then she whipped me. That whipping hurt, but it also felt so good, because my body was so itchy. Every time the belt hit me, it was like a good scratch.

Then, when my grandma came over, I was completely dehydrated. I had scratched holes in my legs and my feet. You know when you run outside after the ice cream truck in the summertime and the bottom of your feet burn? That's how it felt all over my whole body. My tongue had swollen up. I was so dehydrated from vomiting constantly.

My grandma was not having this:

Grandma: "She need to go to the hospital. I'm taking her to the hospital."

Mama: "Don't take her to the hospital. She don't need to go to the hospital. She faking. She faking."

Grandma: "This is why you gonna end up losing these kids."

My grandma ignored her and took me to the hospital. Later on, they told me that if she hadn't brought me in when she did, I would have died that night from dehydration alone.

I had toxic shock. That was my first time getting a Pap smear. I was thirteen. They had to break my hymen, all that shit. Two people stuck their finger in my butt. It was the worst.

But there was this sexy doctor that came in. I'll never forget that doctor. He was black and really strong and he was scary handsome. He was pressing on my stomach and stuff.

Doctor: "Does that hurt?"

I would try to be all sexy and cute, and say it seductively.

Tiffany: "Owwww yes . . . it hurts. Owwww."

It really did hurt, but I was trying to be cute about it. He left the room, but I wanted him to come back. I wanted him to come back, because I thought he was so handsome.

Tiffany: "I need the doctor. I need the doctor."

Nurse: "What's the matter?"

Tiffany: "It's hurting. It's hurting so much in my lower stomach and in my area. It's hurting."

Nurse: "You sure? Here, I can give you some pain medicine."

Tiffany: "No, I think the doctor needs to come back in here."

Nurse: "He's still on the floor. We'll get him to come back."

I fixed my hair and spread it out on the pillow, made it look seductive. I was thirteen, and I was so stupid. I was trying to make it look sexy.

When he came back, I threw the sheet to the side and I opened my legs and said:

Tiffany: "I think I need another thing where y'all check with the thing 'cause it hurts a lot. I think you need to look at it."

He threw the sheet back over me.

Doctor: "Miss Tiffany, that's very cute but you do not need to be looked at down there anymore. You're going to be just fine. I just looked over all your lab reports and everything is getting back to normal very quickly. You'll be out of here by tomorrow. Okay? Nobody needs to look at your private parts anymore."

Tiffany: "Are you sure?"

Doctor: "Yes, I am quite sure."

Oh my God, I was a thirsty kid.

Controlling, Jealous Boyfriends

Every boyfriend I get is jealous. Every man that I date is jealous of other people around me or jealous of me. I don't know what it is about me. I got to figure that out.

I can't tell you how many guys I've dated who are all about, "No phone calls from dudes. Who is this dude? What's his name? What kind of business is it? Are you cheating on me? Are you cheating on me? Blah blah blah blah blah."

So many of these guys fussing at me every single day about dudes. Do they not realize I'm in a male-dominated business, and I'm going to have to talk to men every day? That's just a part of my gig. I try to explain this, then I hear, "Well you shouldn't be flirting. You shouldn't be sending emojis."

When I did this television special one time, I got two, three hundred text messages from all these different comedians. The guy I was dating went through my phone and deleted a bunch of them.

I let him do it, because I have nothing to hide. I don't know why guys do that, but they always look at my phone. Every guy that I've dated has gone through my phone.

But I can't even get mad at the dudes who are jealous and possessive. You know why?

I'm picking them.

I pick every dude. I literally walk up to them, grab their arm, like, "You are beefy. What's your name? You sexy."

That didn't work in high school. In high school dudes were like, "What? What is wrong with you? You talk to Tiffany? What's wrong with Tiffany?"

It works now. Now guys respond.

Well, at least the guys I tend to be attracted to—possessive and jealous and controlling—they respond.

The good guys, they don't as much. They get scared.

One of my comedy buddies tried to help me:

Comedy Buddy: "Tiffany, you need to just smile and don't say shit. Look at the dude. Smile and then look away. If they like you, they going to come for you. You're a beautiful girl. You should never say, 'Damn, you look beefy' or 'You're handsome.' You don't need to do that."

For most guys, I think he is right. For most guys, if a woman approaches them, they don't know how to process it.

If you're a woman and you compliment a guy, even something simple like, "Oh, nice shoes," and you don't work with them every day, you're not seeing them every day, it's just some guy you meet and you compliment them—they think something is wrong with your pussy. They think, even subconsciously, that your pussy must be broke.

That's why so many guys tell me, "You be acting thirsty." Comedy Buddy always says this:

Comedy Buddy: "You act like you're an ugly girl. You're like an ugly girl inside of you, but a pretty girl on the outside. Did you know that?"

It's like fat people who lose weight, in their head, they're still that fat person they used to be.

The other day, I was thinking about why I am like this. I think I act like this, and I end up picking jealous and possessive guys, because in some sick, twisted way, I think that means they care. I'm like, "Look at all the energy he's putting into finding out what I'm doing."

The reality is, in my life, no man's ever really cared. As a kid, I didn't have any man that cared about me.

My dad didn't care. Stepdad didn't care. Uncles didn't care. Nobody cared.

I think that I interpret possessiveness from men as love.

Also, my grandma said to me as a child:

"Every man is going to think of you as property. That's why they want to put they last name on your name. Then you're their property. So you want to make sure whoever you end up with knows how to maintain their property. See yourself as a house. You have to view yourself as the house on the highest part of the hill. You can't let everybody come into your house. They can't catch no bus to your house. They can't ride no bike to your house. They got to have a nice car with four-wheel drive to get up to your house."

Ain't that some fucked up shit to say to a little girl? Especially a poor girl, who was in and out of foster care?

The reality is, for all of my twenties, I thought of myself as an apartment in the projects. Right in front of the bus stop. "Who wants some? Who wants to come in the apartment, hey! Let's have a party. Who wants to be in here?"

I just wanted anyone in. I would let anyone in who wanted to guard this property. To protect me. If you understand that about me, you understand why I was with the wrong men so long.

I know I've got to stop it, though. I'm single now. I am just going to kick back and see what comes to me. I'm not going to keep repeating these patterns with men. They are not working.

The Ex-Husband

I just got to warn you straight up: this story is bad.

And not bad in a funny way, like the Roscoe story, or the Titus story. Like, this is just flat-out bad. This story is probably going to frustrate you. It might even get you angry.

I almost did not put this in the book. I mean, there isn't much here that's funny, to be honest. But I ended up putting it in, because of three reasons:

1. It's the hard truth about my life. I will always tell the truth, even when it's not fun.

2. I hope some young girls can learn from my mistakes and avoid what I went through.

3. I believe everything happens for a reason, and as bad as this was, I believe it's made me better and helped me get where I am.

With that in mind, lemme tell you about my experience with marriage, domestic violence, and self-delusion.

It all started when I went on that cruise with Titus. The one where he brought $50 for the whole cruise? That one.

On the plane, I met this guy who was a cop. I ain't even going to say his real name, it don't matter. I'll just call him Ex-Husband. Me and Ex-Husband talked for a while, and he seemed nice. It turned out he was going to the same cruise I was, and he wanted to take a cab with me there.

But I had Titus, and I wasn't all that into this guy. But he was a policeman, and I thought, *This will be a good friend to have.* It's always good to have police friends, especially black police, because there aren't a lot of them.

You already read about all the nonsense that went on with Titus. Well, I left some details out of that story, because I knew I was going to tell them here. Part of the reason Titus was so upset was because of Ex-Husband.

This dude was straight following me around the cruise the whole time. Like everywhere I was at, he was there. And he always had a video camera filming everything. Like I was singing karaoke, he was filming that. I would be in like a shuffleboard contest, he's filming that. Ping-Pong, he was filming that. We was swimming in the pool, me and my boyfriend, like hugging on each other, he's filming that.

Titus got in an argument with me, started yelling and cursing at me, because this man was following me around with a camera.

Titus: "Are you fucking this guy? Why is this guy following you everywhere with the goddam camera? Who the fuck is this?"

I think Ex-Husband even got *that* on camera. He filmed the argument!

Now, obviously he wasn't standing there filming us like a camera crew would do. That would have been really weird. I wasn't even positive he was filming us, he was sneaky about it. He was always around with his boy and their camera, but I thought maybe he was just filming his vacation. This was back when people did that shit. Everybody was walking around with cameras. Everybody was filming everything. In 2001, that shit was normal.

It all came to a head when I was in the cruise talent show. I was singing James Brown's "Sex Machine," and man, I was into it. I was kinda drunk, so I was gettin' sexy, yelling into the mic, all of that. The crowd loved it.

Titus was in the crowd, and I guess he was getting all anxious about me being sexy, so he runs up to me and throws a jacket around my shoulders, like James Brown.

Then Ex-Husband runs up and throws his boxers and a key to his cabin on the stage. I am serious, the dude took his boxers off somehow, and then threw them onstage.

Well, that changed the whole dynamic.

Titus was hella mad. But he wasn't even man enough to yell at Ex-Husband. He just yelled at me!

Titus: "You fucking him?"

Tiffany: "I didn't even ask that man to do any of that, he just did it himself!"

Titus: "You fucking him, ain't you? Where you fucking him at?"

Tiffany: "Why don't you go ask him?"

Now mind you, Titus came on the boat with $50, so he's highly intimidated. Basically, he's intimidated by Ex-Husband because the dude has a job. And like, money from that job.

Then everywhere we went, Ex-Husband was always trying to do stuff for me. Trying to buy me a drink in the casino. Trying to buy me stuff at the port.

Then Ex-Husband came up to me at the end of the cruise, with Titus standing right there:

Ex-Husband: "Maybe we can exchange numbers or something. I live in Georgia, but you know, I'll call you."

Then Titus be over here talking shit. TO ME! He pulled me aside, yelling at me.

Tiffany: "Why you bitching at me? You don't even say, 'Hey man, that's my girl.' Or whatever, and you want to cuss me out, like yelling at me?"

Titus: "No, you talk to this motherfucker. I've been avoiding them, you tell them. That's your job."

Tiffany: "Fuck you. You acting like a bitch."

I pulled away and gave the dude my number. Titus was pissed off, but you know what, I was pretty much done with him.

Besides, he lived in Georgia. I wasn't never going to see this dude, anyway. I gave him my number mainly because Titus was being such a pussy. We ended up talking on the phone maybe once a month or so. One day I was just like, "Man, you're old." He was like thirty-two. I was like, "You're too old for me," and I hung up.

I ended up changing my number, and I moved and all this stuff, and I didn't even think about him enough to update him. So then he couldn't find me, and I forgot about him mostly.

Five years later, he calls me up out of nowhere. I remembered who he was immediately. We talked for a second, but I was curious how he found me.

Ex-Husband: "Tiffany, I been looking for you for five years. I'm so excited to talk to you again."

Tiffany: "Well if you wanted to talk to me, why didn't you look me up sooner?"

Ex-Husband: "I couldn't spell your last name. Then I saw you on Bill Bellamy's *Who's Got Jokes?* and I saw I was spelling your name wrong."

Tiffany: "Yeah, but my number ain't listed."

Ex-Husband: "Yeah, I know. I got your phone number from a dude I know who works at Sprint. I'm police, that's easy."

After he told me everything he did to find me, I asked him:

Tiffany: "If you could find me, maybe you could find my dad?"

Ex-Husband: "Oh, I'll find your daddy for you, but it's going to cost you."

Tiffany: "I'll pay you whatever you want. Whatever you want, I'll pay you."

In my mind, I'm thinking I'll give him a couple hundred dollars, maybe a couple of dates or something. That's it. Then he's like:

Ex-Husband: "Well, I want you to marry me."

I just start busting up laughing, but he was serious.

Ex-Husband: "Tiffany, I'm telling you, I want you to marry me. I've been watching this video I found, you know, when we was on the boat. Every time I'm sad, I watch you. You make me happy. I don't even really know you, but you've made me happy over the years. When I've had arguments with my girlfriends, I put in our little cruise video, and it just, you know, it makes me happy. I know we weren't on the cruise together, but you were my whole cruise."

I thought it was so cute, but I still wanted to see if he was serious.

Tiffany: "Well, I don't know. If you find my dad, then maybe we could talk about that."

Ex-Husband: "I'm going to find your dad."

I know what you're saying right now, because it's what everyone says at this point in the story:

"That didn't creep you out?"

No motherfucker, it did not!

Now you're probably asking, "Why not?"

That's how you know I'm crazy. Because I literally thought that this call was a sign from God. I thought God had answered my prayers. Just two months before, I was praying to God every day:

"Please send me a man that love me. That care about me. That want to see me flourish. That want to just be there for me, and support me, and do what I want to do. Like just really want me to be happy. Please send me somebody like that."

Then boom, I get this phone call. I was like, *What? Damn God, you work fast. And he gonna find my dad? You awesome, God, I'm in.*

I didn't tell him much about my dad, because I don't know much. I just knew my dad's name, his birthday, and where he came from.

Three weeks went by . . . and my dad called me.

For like ten years, I had been trying to reach him. I'd been looking for him since I was sixteen. I did not think he would find him. And this dude straight found my daddy in three weeks.

I was crying, because I recognized the voice immediately. He started telling me stuff about my family, that only the family would know.

After the call, my mind went racing. God or not, I thought to myself, *Damn, I'm not really going to honor this. I can't really marry this dude. I don't even remember what he looks like.*

He had a Myspace page, and his picture on his Myspace page was so damn little, you couldn't see what this motherfucker looked like. I called him up, still crying after talking to my dad.

Tiffany: "Man I'm so grateful. You found him. I don't know if I can honor our agreement. I don't even remember what you really look like. The pictures you got online is wack."

Ex-Husband: "We going to see each other. We going to see each other."

I didn't believe him. He was across the country from me.

We still kept talking on the phone. I booked a movie in New Orleans like the next day, and two weeks after that I was in New Orleans.

I always talked to him on the phone, but I never told him where I was in New Orleans. I never told him what hotel, the name of the movie, or anything.

At that point in time, I was very superstitious. It was mainly because of Kevin Hart. He gave me this advice as I started to get going:

Kevin Hart: "Don't be telling people everything that you're doing, because motherfuckers will try to make you fail. Just do your shit. You ain't gotta tell everybody you got a movie. Just do the fucking movie, Tiffany. Like don't tell people where you're at, because they're going to come for you. They're going to come for you. Because people will be trying to do bad stuff. They think bad thoughts, and they jealous, and they will try to fuck you up."

So I never told him what the name of the movie was, what kind of part I was playing, nothing. I just said "I'm working," that's it. "I'm working. I'm in New Orleans working."

One night, I was out drinking at the Cats Meow all tipsy, and he called my phone.

Tiffany: "When are you coming to see me?"

Ex-Husband: "I'll come see you right now."

Tiffany: "Yeah, right. You ain't coming to see me."

We got off the phone, and I went back to drinking and didn't think nothing of it. I woke up at five in the morning to start getting ready for the movie. I was hungover and getting ready to go to set. I was braiding my hair in these little crackhead braids, so I could play this drug addict in the movie. I got a knock on my door. I thought, *I didn't order no food.*

I opened the door, and there was a chubby, plain-looking guy in a polo shirt, just staring at me like he was expecting me to say something.

Tiffany: "Who are you?"

Ex-Husband: "It's me. It's Ex-Husband."

Tiffany: "How do you know what room I'm in? How did you know to come here?"

Ex-Husband: "I just looked you up. It's not hard. I called the front desk, they said what room you're in. Here I am."

That motherfucker drove seven hours. He drove all the way from Atlanta for me. And all I'm thinking to myself is, *This motherfucker is ugly.* He's fat. He is not hot, and he is just not very attractive.

Later, he said the same thing to me. He said, "When I first saw you at the door, I was thinking, *This bitch has got skinny. She looks like she on drugs. She wore the fuck out. I'm not feeling this at all.*"

Yeah, but I was TRYING to dress like a crackhead, for the movie. He wasn't trying to be fat and ugly, he just was.

Tiffany: "Well, you can stay in the living room part. You can sleep on the couch. It folds out, if you want to go to sleep. I'm about to go to work."

I went to work, came back to the room. He'd cleaned up the room, bought flowers and stuff. He took me out to a really nice restaurant. The next day, he took me shopping.

He didn't try to fuck me, he didn't try to kiss me or nothing. So I started thinking he was gay, because why you buying me stuff, and taking me to nice restaurants, and not trying to fuck me?

Then he went back to Georgia. The next weekend, I drunk-dialed him, and he showed right back up the next day, and he took me out again. That's when Harry Potter was hot, so I got him to buy me the whole Harry Potter book series. I got him to buy me some stuff from Victoria's Secret. I was like, *If he's gay, he can just buy me everything. Fuck it.*

I don't mind hanging out with gay dudes. I just really thought he was gay. Then the following weekend, it was his birthday.

Ex-Husband: "I'm going to fly you to Atlanta so you can see my house."

Tiffany: "I don't need to see your house. I'm not going to care about your house."

Ex-Husband: "No, I'm going to fly you Sunday. It's my birthday."

He flew me to Atlanta, and that was the first time a man flew me somewhere, so I was feeling super-special, even if he was gay.

At this point, I'd been talking to him seriously for a few weeks, and he'd been buying me stuff and being so nice and flying me places and he even found my daddy. Yeah, he wasn't all that hot, but damn—no man had ever been this good to me.

After he picked me up from the airport, we pulled up to his house. In my little pea-brain, I thought this was the most beautiful house in the whole wide fucking world. I was telling myself, *I don't care if he is gay, I am fucking the shit out of him. He's going to get the business. I don't care if he's gay and ugly and fat, I'm going to fuck him.*

So I did fuck him, and he wasn't gay. It was like my soul had left my body. It was like, *This is your husband, girl. You need to lock this in. He knows what he's doing.* He was all cool.

Then when we were done, I was like:

Tiffany: "So where my ring at? Ain't you supposed to be giving me a ring or something?"

Ex-Husband: "What? You really want to get married? We can do that. We can do that shit today."

Tiffany: "Yeah, I want to get married. I want my ring. It better be pretty and stuff, too."

That day, he drove me up to Virginia to meet my dad. I met my dad in person, and he filmed all that. After I met my dad, we drove back down to Atlanta.

Don't get me wrong—there were signs of craziness during all of this, but I didn't think much of it. I know what you're thinking, *MORE signs of craziness? As in, more than what you've told me?*

Yeah, there were. This is when I confirmed that he wasn't really filming his vacation on that cruise ship. He was just filming me. I only got to see the cruise video one time, but yeah, it was real stalkerish. It's creepy. He was hiding the camera under a jacket, following me around. The camera was pointed at my booty a lot. It was crazy.

But you gotta understand my mind at the time. I'm thinking this is God's work. Like this is exactly what I asked God for, even if he is not all that physically attractive, I can live without that. What's important is his soul, and to me, his soul seemed like it cared about and cherished me a lot.

After that, I flew back to California. He told me:

Ex-Husband: "I'm going to come to California, and we're going to have the best—you're gonna have the best life, the best everything."

The next week, he came out to LA, and he brought me a Dodge Charger.

Ex-Husband: "You can't be driving in no Geo Metro, you drive this."

Tiffany: "Great, cool. I can live with this sort of life."

He drove a Dodge Charger from Atlanta to LA. For me.

Honestly, part of the reason I was looking past the craziness was my own arrogance, in a way. I had started thinking I had the best cootchie in the world. I was thinking, *My pussy is the best pussy ever. There must be midgets in my pussy doing magic tricks on his dick or some shit.* Like, no man had ever brought me cars from other states, so it MUST be something about me.

Turns out, he had a tracking device on that car. He was tracking everywhere I went. He was just watching me, that's why he brought it. He also had one of his former police partners, one of his buddies who lived in LA, watching me. So that dude was following me around when he wasn't in town.

I didn't know any of this, I found all this out later on. Just checking to see what I was doing is what he said. He said he was doing it to keep me safe, but really he was a stalker.

I could have seen the signs then, if I wanted to. For example, one day I didn't answer the phone at all, I just didn't feel like talking, and he just popped up in my house. I thought that was . . . unusual.

I kept telling myself that he did this because he cared about me. But really, he was controlling me. That's what it was about. Not love, not caring, it was about control.

But I either didn't know any better, or I wasn't willing to see it. I looked past his issues, so I could have a man in my life who did things for me.

Even though we were "engaged," he formally proposed to me at a comedy club. I was onstage, and he was going to come up to the stage and give me the ring, but then he got scared for some reason. When the show was over, when nobody was around, he was like:

Ex-Husband: "Will you marry me?"

Tiffany: "Yeah, but why did you wait till nobody was around?"

All my friends was like, "He's ugly, Tiffany, you can do better. Like, he fat. He's ugly. Yeah, he really love you and stuff, but he's wack. Like, you could do better."

I thought they were all haters. I just thought they were jealous or whatever. Because he drove a car out for me, he gave me a ring, and he was giving me an allowance, too. I thought that was super-dope. That's how you know I was stupid. He was giving me like $100 a week, and I thought that was so fucking awesome. I thought that was the shit.

Not that I needed it, but it meant a lot to me. Because to me, if a man cares about you, he gives you money. He works hard for his money, so if he gives it to you, he cares.

So even though all my friends hated him, I just thought they were jealous. And none of them knew all the crazy stuff. At least not yet. But crazy can't hide forever.

He moved out to LA soon after that. And he had a son with him. He told me he had three kids, and he brought his son with him, the eight-year-old.

So now we are living in my one-bedroom apartment. Me, him, and his eight-year-old. I did not like that at all. We only lived there for a month, and then he got this house, and the house was great, but it was far. It was like seventy miles outside LA, in Wildomar.

I thought he was doing it for me. He wasn't. It was to keep me away from everybody and make me feel like I didn't want to do comedy anymore.

But I still kept doing comedy, I just did it in Wildomar. I just found places out there, did the casinos and stuff like that, did shows in San Diego. That shit used to piss him off.

Ex-Husband: "You don't need to do this comedy stuff. I'm making money, you don't need it."

Then as soon as he was saying that, he would lose his job (he was doing private detective work), or get laid off, and so then I had to be supplementing everything. So I started booking movies and all these other really good-paying gigs.

Then as soon as we got married, he had all kinds of demands on me around taking care of his son.

Ex-Husband: "You need to go to the PTA meetings. You need to pick up the kid and take him to soccer."

Tiffany: "Can he go home to his mom for six months, so I can learn how to just be a wife for a little bit? Can I just learn how to do that part for a little bit? Then he can come back, and then I can assume the mommy role? Because this is stressful."

I loved the little boy, but I was instantly being thrown into this mommy role. And honestly, it made me feel like I was nine years old again, taking care of somebody, trying to do my thing, too. I was trying to learn how to be a wife and be a loving partner and all this also.

I was confused as fuck. That was a lot for me, because I was also trying to do my comedy. I was trying to do this for real. And then he told me he don't want me talking about his son onstage, but his son is funny as hell. He's doing really crazy, funny stuff, and I really want to talk about it, and he tells me don't talk about him? Then he tried to tell me not to talk about him, either. But my whole world was those two. What else am I going to talk about?

There was all kinds of stress like that. Basically, he was trying to shrink my world down, until it was nothing but him and his needs. But I wasn't about to let that happen, and I didn't see what he was doing at the time.

Then the relationship got violent.

I was drunk one night, and I just kept saying over and over:

Tiffany: "I want to eat. I want to eat. I want to eat when we get to the house. I can't wait till we get to the house. I'm going to eat that cabbage that you cooked. Oh man, it's going to be so good. I'm about to tear that cabbage up."

Only a drunk person could be excited about eating cabbage, so you know I was drunk as shit.

I honestly don't remember how it happened, but we were in the kitchen, and I was trying to heat up the cabbage, and he choked the shit out of me. He told me I needed to shut up and listen, I talked too motherfucking much, and he choked me.

Now look—we've all been around drunk people we *wanted* to choke the fuck out of. And if I was raving about eating cabbage, then I was probably in that category. But still, it's different to want to choke a drunk person, and to *do it to your wife.*

When he was choking me, at first I was just like, *What the hell?* Like, I could not even believe I was being choked.

Then my survival instincts kicked in.

I grabbed the pan on the stove next to me, and I hit him with it. He dropped his hands, and staggered a bit.

Now that I had my senses, and I could breathe, the rage came.

I threw a vicious right hand and punched him in the eye. That staggered him more, I guess he didn't expect me to fight back.

I grabbed the first thing I could find, which was some pet spray—stuff for the carpet, for pets, you know? I sprayed that in his face. Apparently, that shit don't feel good, because he started covering his eyes and screaming.

I didn't stick around after that, I just wanted to get the fuck out the house.

But as I was running, somehow he caught me and tackled me and sat on me. He closed the door and just sat on me. He sat on me for about forty-five minutes, until I was just not moving or whatever.

He sat on me so long, because I kept fighting. I'd be still for a second, and just like bam, you know, flip out and try to get up out of there.

Ex-Husband: "You need to listen to me. You're disrespectful. You're ornery."

Tiffany: "But you picked me. You married me. You came looking for me. I didn't come looking for you. If you don't like who I am, why the fuck you here? Let me up, and I'll go."

Ex-Husband: "Just shut the fuck up."

But I wouldn't shut up. That ain't my thing, shutting up. He sat on me and lectured me, telling me how fucked up I was as a person or whatever for like an hour. Finally, he got off me, and he dragged me into the guest room and locked me in the guest room.

Ex-Husband: "You're not coming out till you're calm. Bitch, you stay in the holding tank."

I was a prisoner. In my own home.

Ladies, a quick word of advice: that shit is a felony. I did not know it at the time, but someone locking you away without your consent is straight-up kidnapping. A felony. I should have just called the police, but I didn't know that.

He kept me in there till the next day.

Ex-Husband: "Are you ready to be a mature adult now? Are you ready to talk up a conversation like a regular adult?"

Tiffany: "Yeah, let's talk."

He opened the door, and I walked straight out to the bedroom, got out my suitcase, and I started packing my shit.

Tiffany: "You can talk to me while I pack my shit. I'm leaving. I'm out of here. I'm going go to my grandma's house."

Ex-Husband: "Not in my car. You're not taking my car."

Tiffany: "That's okay. I'll take my Geo Metro."

That thing was barely working, but I wouldn't get rid of the Geo.

Tiffany: "I still got my apartment. I'll go back to my apartment with my ornery ass."

Ex-Husband: "No. You don't got to go nowhere. I'm out of here. I'm leaving."

He just got in the car and left. That was easy. Then his mama called me:

Mama: "Why did you send my son home? What the hell?"

Tiffany: "I didn't send him nowhere. Your son choked me. Your son sat on me. Your son locked me up. Your son is abusive."

I took pictures of my throat and stuff and sent them to her.

Mama: "Oh you're a great actress. You're a wonderful makeup artist."

Tiffany: "I ain't no makeup artist. Did you see my makeup at the wedding? I did that myself, and it was horrible, so knock that shit off."

I ended up taking him back. He apologized, sort of, and sent me gifts, and I felt terrible about everything, and we got back together.

I felt like maybe it was my fault, because I was intoxicated. Maybe I wasn't listening. Maybe I was doing too much wrong. So maybe it was my fault. That's how I felt at the time.

I know, I know. You're right. I should not have taken him back. It's easy to sit here now and evaluate this and see I made the wrong decision. I know that.

But it wasn't easy for me, at the time. A lot of women who suffer physical violence go through this. You get in a bad relationship, and you don't—or you can't—find your way out. It's easy to talk about leaving him. It's hard to do it. Part of you really thinks it will get better, and he said it would.

Obviously, it didn't get better.

One night at the Laugh Factory, a bunch of friends from high school came in and saw the show and had a great time. Afterwards, we went next door, and they had drinks. I didn't have any drinks because I had to drive seventy miles home, I just danced around. I got home about 2:30 a.m. and I hadn't called him to tell him I was going to be out with them or anything. He was very upset.

Ex-Husband: "Where the fuck was you at?"

Tiffany: "I was with my high school friends, they showed up to the show to surprise me! Man, it would have been so great if you would have been there."

I was all smiling and happy. He just lifted me up off the ground by my throat.

Ex-Husband: "Don't be standing here lying to me, smiling in my face, telling me you were dancing with some bitches, you a motherfucking liar."

Tiffany: "I'm not a liar, you can look on Facebook. The pictures are on Facebook."

He was choking the shit out of me, my eyes like went red, and I was just looking at him. I didn't try to hit him back or nothing. I was just like . . . I couldn't believe it. I thought to myself, *This is how I'm going to die. I'm going to die, because I was having fun with my classmates.* That's what I was thinking.

Then he just dropped me.

Ex-Husband: "Anytime you just change your mind about what you're going to do, when you get sidetracked, you call me and you tell me where the fuck you at, because I need to know. It is my job to protect you, and you have to tell me where you at, and what the fuck you're doing, because I have to protect you. It's my job as your husband to protect you."

Tiffany: "But I was safe. I felt safe. I didn't need you. I don't need you to protect me."

I slept in the guest room for like two weeks after that. I thought I was going to leave, but I didn't. Once I had taken him back after the first incident, I guess that was it. I accepted that this was part of our relationship.

A few months later, I had to go to Montreal to do the Just for Laughs Comedy Festival. I was scheduled to be there for two weeks. I had a great time the first week. The second week, he came to visit me.

He would not leave my side, and all I wanted to do was hang out with all the comedians down in the lobby. We'd be talking and cracking jokes and stuff, up till like three, four in the morning, just hanging out, laughing, and talking. Dom Irrera was there, and he and Dom were talking, and he basically spent an hour telling Dom how everybody's fake and phony. Saying stuff like he knows they're all trying to fuck me and all this stuff.

Tiffany: "What if they are trying to fuck me? I'm not going to fuck them. They would have to like gang rape me to get me. Like, I'm not going to do that."

Ex-Husband: "Yeah, bullshit, bullshit. You'd probably like it."

Then Tom Green comes over, and he is talking to me and making me laugh so hard. I was just laughing and laughing, and that shit was making my ex-husband so mad. He grabbed me by my collar, he was like, "It's time to go to the room now," in front of everybody. Just snatched me by my shirt, and pulled me to the elevator, and threw me in it.

Jo Koy was in the elevator, and I think Adam Ray was, too.

Jo: "You all right, Tiff? Is everything okay? Are you good? Are you good?"

Ex-Husband: "She's fine. She's just fine. You all stop fucking talking to her. Getting tired of everybody talking to her motherfucking ass."

Tiffany: "I'm okay guys. I'm okay. I'm all right."

I was just trying to make a silly face, trying to be cool, or whatever. Anything to avoid the mortifying embarrassment I was feeling.

Once we got to our hotel room, he was so quick. He snatched me by the neck and slammed me into the wall.

Ex-Husband: "Don't you ever fucking embarrass me like that again. What the fuck is wrong with you?"

I had a knot on the side of my head from where he slammed me into the wall, and all these marks on my throat, where he had dug in his nails. I'd had enough.

Tiffany: "Look, straight-up you need to leave, or I'm going to call the police on you. You're going to go to jail in Canada. I'm going to call the police."

He refused to leave, so I go to grab the phone, and he rips it out of the wall.

Tiffany: "You really need to leave or I'm going to the police. I haven't been to the police before, but there's nail marks on my throat, I'm getting a knot on the side of my head. You need to leave. You really need to go back to California, get the fuck up out of here, because I'm calling the police."

Ex-Husband: "I ain't going nowhere. I ain't going no-motherfucking-where."

Then I just got really quiet, really calm, like just curled up in the corner, just got really quiet. I let him yell at me. He went into the bathroom, and I bolted out the door, down the stairs, and now I was running around the streets of Montreal.

I was running past the other comedians—full-on running. They were calling out, "Yo Tiff, where are you going? What you running for? What you running from?"

I wasn't about to stop and talk to them. I was too embarrassed, too scared, too upset, too fucked up to talk to anyone. I needed help, but I wasn't about to ask for, or take, any.

I roamed the streets of Montreal till about eight o'clock in the morning. Just walking around. Just roaming. Anything I saw that looked like him, I ran down another street. I was tripping. When I got back to the room, about nine o'clock in the morning, he was gone. All his stuff was gone.

During this time in my life, I had dedicated myself to becoming a better wife, so I had started studying with Jehovah's Witnesses. He liked that.

Ex-Husband: "Yeah, I'll never be a Jehovah's Witness, but you should be one, because they know how to be submissive. They're submissive to their men. They do whatever their men tell them to do, so that's what you should do."

The Jehovah's Witnesses do Bible study on Skype. When I got back to my hotel room at nine in the morning, they hit me up on Skype for our regular Bible study.

JW: "What happened to you?"

I hadn't even looked at myself, and when I saw myself on the Skype . . . I saw there was a knot on my forehead, there were all these welt marks across my throat.

Tiffany: "Oh man. My husband came out here, we got into it, he choked me."

Jehovah's Witnesses do not believe in divorce. Not for any reason. They were all like:

JW: "You need to get a divorce. You have to get out of this."

Then the lady leading the Bible study calls her husband. Her husband's an elder, but she gets him on Skype right away.

JW: "Look at Tiffany. Look at her. She needs to get a divorce. Don't you think?"

He is an elder, he is big-time. At first, he started off with the normal lines:

Elder: "Nobody gets divorced. We could talk through this. You could work it out."

JW: "LOOK AT HER FACE!"

He got real quiet. Then he said in a solemn voice:

Elder: "You have to get a divorce. When you come back from Montreal, you're staying with us. You have to get a divorce. You cannot be in a relationship like this. This is not going to work, Tiffany. This man is not godly."

They started reading all the Bible scriptures to me about it. I was crying and stuff, and I had a show to do in a few hours.

Tiffany: "I really need to take a nap. I got a show."

I went to sleep.

I woke up confused about where I was. I had forgotten that I got my ass whipped by my husband. My reflection in the mirror was a shock.

I put makeup on my neck and pulled my bangs over the knot on my forehead.

When I got to the stage, the lights were unexpectedly bright. They were hot. When my makeup started running, everyone there could tell I had been beaten. They could see the marks.

But everybody knew already, they didn't need to see the marks. Those comedians around the elevator and lobby told everybody.

Everywhere I went, people would ask me, "You all right? We heard you got beat. Are you okay? You need help?"

I told everyone I was good.

But I wasn't good. I was in a bad way. All those people there wanted to help, but I couldn't receive their help. All I could do was push them away, and then go back to the dude that was abusing me.

Why?

I ask myself that a lot. I don't know the answer. Maybe because I didn't want to be a quitter. I felt like it was my first time making a commitment in front of God, and getting married was a big deal to me. I'd never been baptized or anything like that. So this was the biggest commitment that I'd ever made in my life, and I didn't want to be a quitter, I wanted to find a way to make it work. I didn't want to seem like I just gave up.

Even though I got beat up. Even though the Jehovah's Witnesses were telling me to get out. Even though a different pastor, from the Baptist Church, was also telling me to get out. It was like God was sending me all these messages to get the fuck out, but I still couldn't.

Maybe it was just that I didn't know any other way to be loved. Maybe this was the only man that I had ever thought truly loved me. Maybe I just couldn't leave that, no matter how bad it was.

I don't know. It's still hard to think about this.

On some level, I felt like if I loved him enough, I could heal him. I could heal him from being mad, from being so vicious.

It was like those *Twilight* movies. It was the same thing for me. I can keep him from drinking human blood. I can bring him deer blood, I can heal him. I just have to love him the right way. I just have to figure out his language, learn how to speak his language.

I even went and talked to his mama:

Tiffany: "How did you show him that you loved him?"

Mama: "Girl, once I burned him with a hot comb, because he was messing with my butt."

Tiffany: "Okay, so I need to burn him with a hot comb?"

Mama: "He was a terrible child. I had to lock him in the house and tell him don't touch nothing until I get back from work."

That was not good advice. So how do I do this? I just really wanted to be a great wife.

Really, I wanted to be a better wife than my mom was.

I wanted to be supportive, not a pushover. But actually take care of the kids, actually take care of people. If I say I'm going to do something, to do it, to have it done. Just better than how she was to me. I wanted to clean the house. Make sure my man don't have no roaches in his house. My mom had roaches in the house. We would never have a roach issue, thank you very much.

So I recommitted. And things got worse at home. He set down new rules for me.

Ex-Husband: "You're not allowed to get text messages or phone calls after ten o'clock, because that's disrespecting our marriage. I don't care if your grandma can't call you after 10 p.m., I don't care if somebody died, that's disrespecting our marriage."

I went along with that. I made everybody talk to me between nine and five o'clock. Business hours. I legit told that to people.

Even though I'm a comedian, and sometimes clubs would be like, "Hey, can you come and do this spot?" I didn't answer the phone. I didn't talk to them. I told them, "I can't do it. I can't do it. If you don't call me during business hours, I can't talk."

Finally, the tide started to turn. I started to see the light. But it wasn't because of anything physically abusive he did to me. More abuse did come, but the last straw was something very different.

One night, we were driving away from the Laugh Factory, and he got a text message. His phone was in the center console, and it popped up on the screen.

Lisa: "Why you be lying?"

I saw that and I knew. Before I even knew, I knew.

Tiffany: "Who is Lisa?"

Ex-Husband: "What are you talking about? You're seeing things."

Tiffany: "No. No. No. Who is Lisa, and why does she say you've been lying?"

Ex-Husband: "You tripping. You seeing things. Something wrong with your eyes."

Tiffany: "Oh, now I'm blind?"

Ex-Husband: "You know you can't read."

Tiffany: "No, I can read now, and this says Lisa: *'Why you be lying?'"*

Ex-Husband: "No. You tripping."

I grabbed the phone, and I started texting her: *"Why?"* She texts back in two seconds, like she's a professional text messager.

Lisa: *"Because you said you was giving me some money to get my nails and hair done tonight."*

I texted back, and I read my message out loud, " *'Well you know my wife be spending up my money.'*"

As I texted that back, he got so mad. He grabbed me by the head and pushed my head into the window. He was trying to get the phone, and I was pulling the phone back.

Tiffany: "Nigga, what is wrong with you? Like what the fuck is wrong with you? What did I tell you about putting your motherfucking hands on me? Get your motherfucking hands off of me!"

Then he pulled over, and he took the phone from me.

Tiffany: "Why you don't want her to know that your wife's spending your money? What's up with that? What's up with that? What's up with that? What's up with that?"

When we black women repeat our words, you know shit is bad. Well, shit *was* bad.

Ex-Husband: "You need to shut the fuck up."

Tiffany: "No. You need to shut the fuck up. I told you to keep your motherfucking hands off of me, and you put your hands on me, and you know what's going to happen. When we get where we got to go, somebody's getting their ass beat, and it ain't going to be me."

I poked him in the side of the head. When I poked him in the side of the head, he went ballistic.

Ex-Husband: "I'm not afraid to fight no one, and I'll pull your ass out the car."

Tiffany: "Pull me out the car, motherfucker."

He waited until we got home, and then it was basically an MMA fight. Except he was big and trained in hand-to-hand combat by the police academy, and I was small and fighting for my life.

He choked me a bunch of times. I scratched at him, I ran from him, all of that. I hit him, but my punches didn't do shit. He's a big guy. I hit him as hard as I could with a pool stick a few times (I found that in the back of his car). He grabbed me by the throat and threw me into a shelf at one point. It was like being tossed around by the Incredible Hulk. I thought my eye socket was broke. My lip was busted. I was tore up.

I am glossing over all the details, because they don't matter. The point was, the man whipped me. He beat my ass.

But now, shit was different. I was done taking this. I was ready to commit murder. I was ready to kill. I got in my car and left the house, and I drove to the police station.

First the police station was closed when I got there. I'm like, What the fuck? How can a police station be closed?

They had an emergency phone outside the front door, so I picked it up:

Operator: "Yes? May I help you?"

Tiffany: "I'm about to kill somebody. I'm about to commit motherfucking murder."

Operator: "Excuse me?"

Tiffany: "I'm out here at the police station. Y'all need to lock me up, because I'm about to kill my husband. If y'all don't lock me up right now, there's gonna be a dead body."

Operator: "Where are you?"

Tiffany: "I'm outside the police station, so y'all could lock me up, 'cause I'm about to make a murder."

Operator: "Don't go anywhere. I'm gonna have one of the officers come out."

The policeman comes out.

Police: "Ma'am, what happened to you? Are you okay?"

Tiffany: "I'm fine. I'm just fine."

Police: "Do you need us to call you an ambulance?"

Tiffany: "No, I'm just fine. I'm about to go make murder."

Police: "You're gonna what?"

Tiffany: "Make a murder."

Police: "Okay. Calm down. Tell us what happened."

So I tell him and his partner what happened. The whole time, they were looking me up and down.

Police: "Okay . . . you do realize that you're very damaged?"

Tiffany: "I am fine. I am just fine. I'm telling you, you need to put me in a jail cell, because I hit that motherfucker with a pool stick, and I'm gonna go back and kill him, if y'all don't lock me up. I'm going to commit murder. I'm gonna go to the hood, get a gun, and I'm gonna kill that motherfucker."

Police: "Ma'am, you need an ambulance. You are hurt."

Then, the other policeman started pulling out his camera. Started taking pictures of my face and my throat. He asked to see my arms. They were all messed up, with cuts and scrapes.

Tiffany: "I didn't even know that happened. Look, I'm gonna kill that motherfucker."

Police: "Calm down. Are you hurting anywhere else?"

Tiffany: "My back hurt when he slammed me in the ground."

Police: "Let me see your back."

When they pulled my shirt up, it was all black and blue. They took pictures of that.

Then, they had an ambulance come. I got in an argument with the paramedics.

EMT: "We need to take you to the hospital."

Tiffany: "No, I need to go to jail. 'Cause I'm gonna go crazy on this motherfucker. I'm fine."

EMT: "Your blood pressure's really high. You need to calm down."

Tiffany: "I don't give no fucks. I'm gonna kill this man."

Finally the police decided to go to my house.

Police: "Look, we have to go see him. If he's injured, if he has damage on him, then you may end up in jail."

Tiffany: "You might as well take me there now. You might as well just start taking my fingerprints now, because I'mma kill that motherfucker."

They took me to the hospital, and went to get him. The police told me later that he was in the house with the door wide open. He was sitting there with his shirt off, watching a football game. He knew they were coming. The police arrested him, 'cause all he had was one bite mark on his wrist. I don't even remember biting him. He didn't have no other marks on him. Nothing.

Tiffany: "No. I hit him with a pool stick, y'all. It should be a big ol' bruise across his back. I hit him with that pool stick as hard as I could."

Police: "Ma'am . . . he was fine."

They arrested him. Then his whole family started calling me. They asked me to bail him out.

Mama: "He wants to know if you'll bail him out."

Tiffany: "I'm not bailing him out! No. I'm getting a restraining order and everything. You crazy if you think I'm finna bail him out."

Then, the next day I was hurting so bad. My back, everything. I could barely walk.

I started bleeding like crazy. From my vagina. When the blood starting coming, I knew. I mean, I didn't know I was pregnant before, but now I did. I was having a straight-up miscarriage. I don't know if it was from the beating or the stress, but it happened.

I guess God decided to send me a real fucking clear sign this time, didn't he?

That was pretty much the end of that. I filed for divorce and moved back into my old place.

Let's just all pause here and take a breath. Maybe get a drink, rest up. Because the story is not done, and we about to dive back into some intensity.

OK, you rested? Here we go:

I left him, but I don't know what the fuck was wrong with me, because *I still wanted my husband back.* Even though I had a restraining order and everything, it was still a part of me like, *I think we can work through this.*

My friend had the same reaction you are having: "Girl, you crazy. This motherfucker almost killed you. Leave him alone."

I just thought . . . he had to see how much he hurt me. He saw how messed up I was. We had love. He'd never do that again. I know he can be a better person. We just got to get some counseling. We can get through this. We got to do this together. We just got to work together. No relationship is easy. It's just work. We just gotta work at it.

I didn't act on these thoughts. I just had them, all through the divorce (which was quick and easy and painless) and afterwards.

After the divorce . . . everything sucked.

I was single now, but I didn't want to be out there dating. Dudes would try to talk to me, but I just wanted my husband. That's all I wanted.

During this time that we were apart, his son went into foster care. Why that happened isn't part of my story, but it did happen.

He was in the foster system for six months.

This really hit me hard. I was in the foster system, I knew how terrible it was. Even though I was divorced from his dad, I was actively trying to help get him out of there. I wanted him to be with his mom or even with me. I even helped his mom to fly out, and I was driving her around.

When I think back about it, I was so fucking stupid with that. That whole situation drove me back toward my ex. It's just my opinion, but I'm convinced he used that situation—that his son was in foster care, and the guilt *he knew* that would cause with me—to try to get me back with him. He knew I'd been in foster care, he knew I would not be able to resist helping his son, and that it would bring me back around him more.

And it worked.

I won't get into more details. You would just start yelling at this page you're reading, like some crazy person.

We got married. Again.

We got a bigger house, a better house. And the one good thing was that me and his son were super-close. His son knew what I had been through with foster care and all this stuff. He was lovin' on me and everything.

And honestly, it was okay for a while. He wasn't hitting me or none of that.

Then he started acting really weird. He started being on the phone for like two, three hours at a time, ducking off into his office. Running into the backyard to talk, being really secretive and stuff.

I tried to have positive thoughts. I'd go on the computer and look through our wedding photos, to remember the good times.

And then one time, I was going through the wedding photos, and there was a photo of a buck naked chick sucking on her titties, in the middle of our wedding photos. That led to a big fight. Nothing physical, just yelling.

I was working on a movie then, and I called him the next day, but couldn't find him. I came home, because I had been a little mean to him in the morning. So I thought, *I'll come home during my lunch break. I'll butter him up like, "I'm sorry for being mean to you this morning."* But, he was not at home when I arrived.

Instead, there was an eviction notice on our door.

Tiffany: "Why hasn't the rent been paid? Why are we getting an eviction notice?"

Ex-Husband: "Because I have a child. I've been talking to her every day. I have to pay $2500 a month. They're garnishing my check. That's where the money is going."

That's why he was asking me for $1000 every month. He said it was going towards the rent. Turns out, he was paying child support. He had another child who was eleven, a little girl, who he basically abandoned, because he didn't like her mom.

It's funny, because a few months before, his mom was at the house, and she was telling me that he got a daughter. But she was drunk, and he was like, "You can't listen to her. She drunk. Don't listen to what she's saying." But, I should've listened.

I had real issues about this.

Tiffany: "Why would you do that? You found my dad for me. And you know how I feel about that. You would just abandon your child? You just let her be out there like that? And then you didn't even tell me that you reconnected with her or that you was paying child support or that you got a court order garnishing your check? You didn't tell me none of that?"

He didn't have nothing to say. I was like:

Tiffany: "Fuck this shit. I'm done. I'm out."

So, I moved out. I got a divorce.

And this time, it stuck. We're still divorced, and we ain't never getting back together.

I know what you're thinking: *This was your breaking point? And not the ass-whippings?*

It seems like a really small thing, relatively. Compared to everything else.

But the thing is, I couldn't be with anybody, or potentially have a child with somebody, who could abandon his child. That was my personal boundary, and I had finally found it.

He had trouble letting go. He kept texting, *"I want my wife back."* He'd be calling my friends. To this day, he still calls my friends. And he's like, "How's my wife doing? I miss her. She's still my wife. Even though we're divorced, she's still my wife."

No, we ain't divorced. We twice divorced.

The Long Road to Comedy Success

I don't want to make comedy sound easy, because it is NOT.

After I got back into comedy, and got my first paid gig ("The Lesbian Bomb Show"), I started doing a lot of paid shows all over LA. Occasionally, I was getting out of town to Orange County or Colton, or something like that, or far off, like Lancaster.

Back then, I considered a two-hour drive to be a serious traveling gig. I wouldn't now, but then I was driving a little Geo Metro that sounded like a lawnmower. Ride in that shit for two hours, you feel like you done crossed America in a covered wagon.

Right as I was getting going with comedy, I kind of blew up in the Bar Mitzvah scene. So I was traveling all over the country, doing Bar Mitzvahs. That paid better than my comedy gigs, but comedy was my thing.

Then I got on the show *Who's Got Jokes?* and that helped my career a lot. It was my first time ever being on television doing stand-up, and I won the first round of competition.

I had to go to Atlanta, and I had never done comedy in Atlanta before. I'd only partied in Atlanta, so I really didn't have a feel for the comedy scene. I didn't know how they even felt about women comedians, or anything. I didn't have a clue. That shit matters a LOT in comedy, and because I was not ready for the second round in Atlanta, I lost bad.

It was in a civic center. There were like three thousand people there, and it was my first time being in front of that many people. And right as I walked out onstage, I realized, *Tiffany, there are motherfucking cameras here.*

I was just so nervous, it was horrible.

At the time, I had this goofy bit about the song "Chicken noodle soup, chicken noodle soup, chicken noodle soup and the soda on the side." I would make fun of that song, do this goofy dance. I did that bit, but I screwed the timing up bad.

I knew I had fucked up. It was so quiet in there. And nobody made a sound. And then some man just went:

Man: "Booo!"

Just out of nowhere. He didn't even yell, it was more dismissive. And because none of the other three thousand people were making a sound, it echoed all around that hall.

I looked into the audience, and all I could say was one word into the mic, real slow and serious:

Tiffany: "Niggas."

That's all I could say. I could get nothing else out of my mouth.

I got disqualified. This wasn't a black comedy club, and you can't say that shit on TV. I was done. I failed. It was bad.

First, I cried. I cried outside in the back of the civic center, hard. Then I started talking to myself and was like, *You just bombed in front of all them people, all over TV. People are gonna be able to see that all over the world.*

Then I responded to myself, *Yeah, people gonna see me, though, all over the world. Then, my daddy gonna see me, and then he gonna come visit me, and then life is gonna be great.*

I was trying to make myself feel better, and I did feel better.

Even though I bombed, getting to the second round helped my career. I did some stand-up on a couple of late night TV shows, and then I ended up doing HBO's *Def Comedy Jam*, and then *Def Comedy Jam* started getting me other shows.

Then I got a movie with Mike Epps, and that started getting me to colleges. It's kind of full circle, 'cause NYU wanted to charge me $30,000 a semester to attend, and now, I'm going to all these different colleges, and they're paying me $2000 to tell jokes for like forty-five minutes. I felt like the dopest person in the world. I was getting paid to go to school. I wasn't really learning anything, but still.

Once I got divorced, it was like the floodgates opened. The quality of my comedy just got way better. I had more time to focus on the art of it, and I was getting to know myself better. I was paying attention to my feelings about things.

In stand-up, you do need to be having fun up there like Richard Pryor said, but you have to know yourself well, too. You have to know when you make different faces, or do different things, you get certain reactions. You start learning and it's like playing a piano. You just know exactly what keys to stroke, 'cause really with comedy, you're like fiddling with people's souls. You resonate on the same frequency as them, trying to get them to relate.

To do that, you gotta put yourself out there. And in order to put yourself out there, you've gotta have an idea of who you are and how people react to that.

A lot of shows during this time stick out in my memory. I did a show in Arizona that was sold-out, and the thing that I remember the most about it was this lady sitting in the front row. She had this mean face. She was mean-mugging me the first ten, fifteen minutes of my set.

I made it my mission to make her laugh, and she would not laugh. It took me like twenty minutes to get her to laugh, and once she did laugh, though, she laughed so hard that snot flew out of her nose. After the show, I went out and danced all night in celebration. I was so proud of myself.

Another time, in the middle of the show, the heel on my shoe broke. So I just did like ten minutes about my shoe, how cheap the shoe was, why the shoe broke, all that. When I came off the stage, this lady came up to me.

Lady: "You were amazing. I peed on myself. I peed on myself."

Tiffany: "Oh, thank you. How many kids do you have?"

You know, because women be peeing themselves after they have babies.

Lots of bad shows, too. I used to host this room at the San

Manuel Casino every Wednesday night, and this one night, a girl was definitely intoxicated. She kept talking through everybody's set, and I was hosting the show. I kept saying, "Watch yourself. Let everybody enjoy the show. You need to be quiet. Calm down." After the third comic, she started again, and it went off.

Drunk Girl: "Yo, is this guy gonna be funny? Them others was stupid!!!"

Tiffany: "Look, I'm getting tired of you talking to people all disrespectful, and if you don't quit, you're gonna have a problem."

Drunk Girl: "Bitch, *you're* gonna have a problem, bitch."

I went the fuck off. She started gangbanging, throwing up signs and talking crazy, so I started banging back. I ain't even from no gang, but I start representing my old hood.

Drunk Girl: "Don't trip. I'll beat your ass right now, in front of everybody."

Tiffany: "Come on. Come, beat my ass, bitch!"

At first, people were laughing, 'cause they thought I was just playing. Then I pulled my hair off. I took my shoes off, I took my earrings off. I balled up my fist, all furious, and I started praying into the microphone:

Tiffany: "Heavenly Father, give me the strength and the power to beat this girl down to the ground, and teach her she ain't never supposed to be this disrespectful to anybody, because I give zero fucks, Lord. Just give me the power to whip her ass. All these things, I ask in the name of Jesus Christ. Amen."

I guess it was the way I said it, because people stopped laughing.

By the time she got close to the stage, security had grabbed her. Then two big Samoan chicks, who used to come every single week, came down right behind her. And then, these other two black girls that came all the time, they started whaling on her. Security had to drag that girl out, to stop her from getting killed. I was yelling from the stage:

Tiffany: "Bitch, getting your ass beat before you even get to the stage. We beating yo ass right now!!"

Everything got settled, and I introduced the headliner. Poor guy, how's he gonna follow that shit? And I was so embarrassed. I had prayed out loud, in front of everybody, for the Lord to give me strength to whip a girl's ass. It was so unprofessional. I was so embarrassed that I went so ghetto, so fast.

When I left from the show, I walked to the police car in the parking lot. It was the car that was taking her to the station, and she was sitting in the back. She was like a rabid dog—mad, face up against the glass, yelling and cussing, and I was like, *damn. That was an hour ago, and she's still crazy like that?*

Another really bad night was when I was supposed to host this April Fool's show in Atlanta. This place held three hundred people, but there was only thirty people there, and they didn't pay me all my money. I only got half my money, and I had the worst set ever.

They had me thinking it was gonna be so many people, but only thirty people showed up. And then, half of them were my ex-husband's family members, so it was very embarrassing. And I don't embarrass easily, obviously. His mom was there, and she was just staring me in the face. It was a horrible show.

Then I fell on the stage. It was bad. I was wearing these pants that looked like leather, but weren't leather, and I was trying to do this physical joke, where I squat down, like a dance, and then pop back up. I squatted down, and when I popped back up, I slipped and fell, so then my little fake leather pants tore a hole on the knee.

I was trying to play it off like it wasn't bothering me, and then, two minutes after I fell, I just kicked my shoes off. I just sat on the floor of the stage.

I just gave up. I just sat on the floor, and just talked from the floor, just finished my time from there. I think I had twenty-five minutes left. It was horrible.

No one laughed. People were rolling their eyes. Looking at me crazy. Nobody was laughing. It was not good.

Afterwards, my ex-husband came up to me:

Ex-Husband: "That set, you get a D on that set."

Tiffany: "I give you an F on being a husband. So suck on that."

I did a bad show at Howard (a black college) with Tony Rock as the headliner, and me as the featured act. It was like, four thousand black students.

I knew immediately this was going to be a problem. I had never seen this many black young people in one place, ever in my life. In one room, I've never seen it. I don't know why that freaked me out, but it did.

I just tried to stick to my material, just do my material, and it was not hitting. I was too nervous and too scared and they were not feeling me at all. At first, it was real quiet, 'cause they tried to figure it out. I don't even remember the first joke I hit 'em with, but it didn't hit at all. That was horrible.

I did the punchline, and nobody laughed, and I just was looking like a deer in the headlights. This one dude from the audience spoke up.

Guy: "It's all right, though, you fine. At least you look good."

Tiffany: "You got that right. Some of y'all get a female comic, and she don't be funny, and she be ugly, too. At least I ain't ugly."

And then one of the girls sitting next to him said in a real bitchy voice:

Girl: "Yeah, *whateva*."

They were all on their phones, chilling there, giving attitude. That chick, she was just on her phone the whole time, just texting. She was sitting right in the front, so I could see her real good. If I saw her in the streets today, I would *still* know her right away.

I was supposed to get paid $2500 for that show, and when I came off the stage, they had already called my manager. My manager called me fifteen minutes after I got off the stage, and he was like:

Manager: "They're only gonna give you $500 for this show. They said it was pretty bad."

Tiffany: "Yeah, it was pretty bad. I'm cool with that."

I started laughing. I sucked, and I still got $500 though. I might have been embarrassed in front of four thousand people, but I can pay my light bill, get groceries, gas money. I'm good.

This is how I know I REALLY sucked: there was an after-party, and the student that was in charge of activities, when we first got there before the show, he was like:

Student Host: "Yeah, you gotta come to the after-party. It's gonna be so much fun. Tiffany, you definitely gotta be there. Everybody's gonna be so excited to see you."

And then, after the show, that dude came and talked to Tony Rock:

Student Host: "Yeah, so the party's gonna be hype. We're gonna pick you up from your hotel in about one hour. It's gonna be great. We got bitches. We got booze. You gonna love it."

And then he looked at me, rolled his eyes, and walked the fuck out of there.

Tony Rock: "Ooo, nigga."

Tiffany: "What?"

Tony Rock: "Yep, your ass really was bad. You're not invited to the party, Tiff."

Tiffany: "He didn't say I couldn't come to the party."

Tony Rock: "That look said you can't go to the party."

Tiffany: "Well, I don't want to go to the stupid-ass college party anyway. I'm an adult."

How about that shit—a twenty-year-old college dude didn't want me at his party!

And then, this little fat girl brought the money in. She handed everyone their envelopes, and she looked like she did not want to give me my envelope. My little $500. She did not want to give it to me. I know I did bad that night, but I got my money, though.

The Politics of Comedy

At this point, I'm pretty well established in comedy and know most of the people and players. But man, it was not like this at the beginning. I've got so many stories about what it was like coming up as a black woman in comedy in LA. Where do I start?

Lemme start with this one comedian. We'll call him "Fats." I was volunteering at the youth center, and I ran into him there. He mentioned to me that he surfs.

Tiffany: "You surf? You don't surf."

In case you don't know, Fats is fat as hell. Three hundred pounds, at least.

Fats: "Yes I do, I surf."

Tiffany: "Wow. I bet you be looking like a sea lion out there in that wet suit and everything."

Fats: "What'chu talkin' 'bout? I got my own line of wet suits and my own line of surfboards."

Tiffany: "Is they plus-sized? That would make sense."

Fats: "NO! THEY AIN'T NO DAMN PLUS-SIZED!"

Tiffany: "Wow. That's pretty amazing. You know, I surf too. I take kids surfing every summer."

Fats: "Oh, maybe I'll donate some surfboards. Here's my number. Give me a call sometime."

So I gave him a call, but every time I called him about the surfboards and stuff, he don't want to talk about that:

Fats: "So you think we can go out to dinner? What do you like to do for fun?"

Tiffany: "You trying to date me or give me the surfboards? I want the surfboards, I don't want to date you."

Fats: "Yo, if you ain't trying to go out with me, I ain't trying to give out no surfboards."

I may have my issues, but I ain't hooking up with some fat ass for free surfboards. Hell no.

Then I ran into him at the comedy club, and he saw me get onstage and demolish it. Everything was different after that. Now he treats me like I'm one of the homies. Like I'm a fellow colleague.

I love that, and now he's a good friend of mine. He ain't trying to take me out to dinner or nothing like that. He respects me as a comedian.

Which before, he probably just thought I was one of them chicks saying I do comedy, trying to get pregnant by somebody rich. 'Cause some girls do that out here.

I had something worse happen with another comic I've decided not to name. I'll call him Rumpelstiltskin. I knew him, because some of my friends opened for him when he went on the road.

Tiffany: "Hey Rumpelstiltskin, I would love to open up for you, you should let me open up for you."

Rumpelstiltskin: "I can't take you on the road."

Tiffany: "Why?"

Rumpelstiltskin: "Unless you opening up those legs, you can't go nowhere."

At first, I thought it was just a joke, right? So the next time I asked him, he said the same thing. I was like, *This motherfucker serious?*

Tiffany: "So lemme get this straight. Whoever's on the road with you, open up they legs for you, is what you telling me?"

Rumpelstiltskin: "I ain't no motherfucking faggot. I'm not saying that, I'm just saying that you can't go nowhere, you gonna ruin my marriage. Your type, you too cute and shit, you gonna have to give up some pussy."

Obviously, that was a no go.

Then, after I got on a TV show and a movie, now his manager wants to call me asking if I'll open up for him. And he wanted to pay me $500 for fifteen minutes. Fuck THAT. Rumpelstiltskin was so shocked that I turned down that offer, he called me up himself.

Tiffany: "A minimum, MINIMUM of $2500 for me to open."

Rumpelstiltskin: "Nigga, what is wrong with you? Don't nobody pay that much money for some goddam comedy. Not no female."

Tiffany: "Uh, yes they do. Yes they do. That's what I get paid on a regular basis."

Rumpelstiltskin: "Well, I guess you gonna be headlining this for yourself, you can just go on out there and headline for yourself."

Tiffany: "Will do. You bet."

And then I started headlining some shows and stuff, and I did pretty good. I guess he heard about how good I did, so he called me:

Rumpelstiltskin: "Well, I just want to apologize. Nigga, you out here getting it. You really doing things. I want to apologize. I was wrong the way I treated you."

I thought that was cool of him, to admit he was wrong. Good for him.

But I had to earn that respect.

There was this other guy that pissed me off for a long time. Let's call him "Cry Baby." He's a comedian you have heard of. When I was starting off, like twenty-two years old, I met him at an open mic. He said I had promise, but I needed to hang out with more comedians to get funnier. I was like, *Cool, this guy's trying to help me.*

So he invited me to a taping at one of his shows for BET. Well, that's what he told me it was. I'm thinking he is *on* the TV show. I get there, and it's not his show at all. He was just doing the audience warm-up! After the show, he was all excited.

Cry Baby: "So what did you think?"

Tiffany: "I thought it was pretty interesting, it's cool."

Cry Baby: "You see how I'm the man up there?"

Tiffany: "You not the man, you the audience warm-up. You warm up the audience."

Cry Baby: "Why you talking to me like that, bitch?"

Tiffany: "Why you talking to me like that?"

Cry Baby: "You disrespecting me?"

Tiffany: "You're disrespecting me, what do you want from me?"

Cry Baby: "Girl, you know what I want from you."

Tiffany: "I do know what you want, and guess what? You not my type. Your titties are bigger than mine, I'm not interested, it ain't never going nowhere. So you just need to chill. We comedians, and that's that."

Cry Baby: "Man, fuck you, stupid bitch."

I just kinda laughed it off. I know his feelings was hurt, but whatever.

But he and I were on the same club circuit at the time, and he was a bigger name than me then. So every time I seen him—for five years—he would bump me off of comedy shows.

If I was supposed to go up next, he'd tell the manager of the club, "No, I want to go up." He'd bump me. It got me pissed, but I just held back and waited. I knew my time would come.

Four years later, we were at the Laugh Factory, and the Laugh Factory is my house. I host there, I headline there, it's my home. So he tries to bump me off the show, and they wouldn't bump me.

Cry Baby: "Yeah whatever, Tiffany, you finna go up there and bomb, you 'bout to ruin the whole thing for everybody, you suck. You ain't no real comic."

Tiffany: "Yes I am a real comic, and I'm about to destroy this room, and you gonna have a hard time following me."

Cry Baby: "Please. You 'bout to eat ass, you 'bout to bomb."

Tiffany: "You the only motherfucker be overeating in this bitch."

Right before I went on stage, I prayed to God to make me as funny as possible in this one moment. If I'm never funny again, make me as funny as possible in this one moment, so I can shut this motherfucker up.

I did fifteen minutes, demolished it. I got a standing ovation, six people stood up for me, it was great. I came off the stage, and all the comedians were clapping. They had heard Cry Baby and me yelling at each other back and forth in the VIP area upstairs. So when I came off, they were all clapping for me like, "Yeah, nigga, you killed that, you did that, girl," and I was like, *Yeah I did.* And it was his turn to go up next.

Cry Baby: "I can't believe this shit. You making me eat my words."

Tiffany: "Yep. Eat them. Eat them up like you eat all them free sandwiches."

So then he went up onstage and he bombed, bad. And then he came back upstairs. He came up, gave me a big ol' hug, he was like:

Cry Baby: "Man I am so sorry, Tiffany. Obviously somebody tried to teach me a lesson."

Tiffany: "Yep. God trying to teach you today."

Ever since then, we have been cool. You know how you can tell somebody can't stand you, but you're undeniable, so they can't really hate? That's how it has been ever since. So when I see him, he's always cool, like:

Cry Baby: "Yeah, I see your commercials, I see you doing little shows, I saw you on Oprah channel."

You can tell it's bothering him, but I am always cool to him, because he apologized and made his shit right. And I will always forgive. I may not forget, but I will forgive anyone, if the apology is sincere, and I feel his was sincere.

Comedy is hard for anyone, but women have a different level of hard.

So many promoters try to pull shit on women. I can't tell you how many tried to tell me that to get onstage, I had to get on my back. Hell no!

I see young female comics now, and I can see the same thing happening. Dudes try to take advantage of them, hold a little bit of power over their heads. I see that going on so much, and then I tell them, "Girl, don't let him pull your ho card. You'll get more if you keep your legs closed, trust me. You'll get more stage time, you'll get more performances, just keep your legs closed."

And it's true. It is so funny, 'cause nobody told me that. I saw all these girls fucking all these dudes and getting stage time, and I just felt like I'm probably ruining my career, 'cause I wasn't going to do that.

But those girls aren't doing comedy no more. None of them. Those girls that I started with that slept around, they all got kids or they quit. Or it's "I became a social worker" or "I'm a nurse now." 'Cause they was getting run through, and how long can that go on?

They thought that was the way, and it's not. You can't get your comedy stripes on your back, you got to earn 'em on your own two feet. 'Cause you can't fake funny.

This one promoter, he tried to fuck me, and I said no. So he told everyone he fucked me in a car at the back of the comedy club. He told this lie to everyone.

I found out he was saying all this, and I went straight hood. I stormed into the club he was promoting at, right when all the comics were going to be there:

Tiffany: "What you saying about me? I was in your mother-fucking car? When was this?"

Promoter: "You wasn't in my car."

Tiffany: "Goddam right I wasn't in yo trashy, broke-ass hoop-tie. But you out here telling people that I was in your car, and you fucked me in that car? And that I was terrible in bed?"

Promoter: "No, I said that your attitude is terrible, because somebody trying to be with you and you ain't trying to give nobody the time of day."

Tiffany: "Well these niggas told me that you said that you fucked me in the back of your car. And I'mma tell you right now, you need to keep my motherfucking name out your mouth, or I will have these goons come up here and fuck you up."

And I got all up in his face and I pushed him. Mind you, this dude is like twenty years older than me and probably a hundred pounds heavier than me.

Tiffany: "You'll get fucked up in these streets. Keep my name out your mouth and don't say shit to me."

That was twelve years ago, and to this day, when he sees me at the comedy club and tries to speak to me, I don't say shit to his ass.

I've learned how to handle those types of situations better now, I don't make threats like that anymore. But at that moment, I had to save face. He was a bitch. He spread rumors about people that ain't true, and gossip, and that's not funny. That shit has an impact.

But sometimes, my friends make the threats for me.

One time, this promoter flew me and my friend Marlow up to Seattle. He was supposed to give us our money before we got on-stage. He gave us half our money:

Promoter: "I'm gonna give you the rest when you get off."

We get offstage, we finish the show.

Promoter: "Okay, I'm gonna give you the rest of your money when we get to the hotel."

But we didn't go to a hotel.

Promoter: "Okay, we got to go to a casino right quick, and then I'm gonna take y'all to the hotel."

So we at the casino, he buys us some drinks and runs off, and the next thing we know, it's five o'clock in the morning, our flight's supposed to leave at 7 a.m.

Promoter: "Aw man, can I write you a check?"

He was a reputable promoter, so we said, "Yeah okay, write us a check." So he wrote us a check, dropped us off at the airport. He had printed out our return tickets home. We went to check in, ain't no ticket, ain't no flight, nothing.

There's nothing for us to get home. So we start calling, we blowing up his phone:

Promoter: "What do you mean, there's no ticket? There's a ticket."

Tiffany: "Motherfucker we are not calling you because we want to talk. THERE'S NO FUCKING TICKET. You sure we at the right airline?"

Promoter: "YES! My homegirl work at Southwest, she sets me up, she do everything, that's the only airline I use."

Turns out, homegirl canceled everything. Why? Because she caught him with another bitch the day before. He neglected to mention that shit about his "homegirl."

Marlow was having none of this. I don't know who Marlow called, but the next thing you know, an hour and a half later, the promoter showed up at the airport, and he paid cash for these tickets. And he gave us the rest of our money in cash.

Promoter: "Marlow, please don't have that man call my phone no goddam more. I don't want no problems, and I ain't never booking y'all for nothing again. Please, just leave me alone and let me live my life."

Marlow: "Yeah, motherfucker, we don't never want to do your shit again, treating us like shit 'cause we women. If we was men, you wouldn't treat us like this, motherfucker!"

I never asked Marlow who she called. I just know that Marlow's from Compton, and she knows a lot of motherfucking gangstas. She knows Suge, all them. I don't know who she called, but I will tell you, this promoter had the fear of God in him.

All this shows, it's really hard as a woman in comedy. But I don't want to make it out like all dudes is bad. Some guys are amazing. Like Kevin Hart. He's like, my comedy guardian angel.

There was a time, early in my comedy career, when I was homeless. I was living in the Geo Metro. I used to be homeless in Beverly Hills, and I thought, *If I'm homeless, I'll be homeless with class. Keep my nails done. Keep my hair pretty, baby wipes, I'm fresh, it's okay. I'm in Beverly Hills. As long as I'm sleeping in Beverly Hills, I'm safe.*

I pulled up to the comedy club one night, and Kevin Hart saw all that shit in my car.

Kevin: "What the fuck is going on with you?"

Tiffany: "Nothing. I'm good. I'm just in between houses."

Kevin: "No. What the fuck is going on?"

I told him what was up. I cried and everything, I opened up to him.

Kevin: "Tiff, you can't be living like this. You a pretty girl. Like, you a beautiful woman. Why are you living in your car? Any dude will be happy to let you live in his house."

Tiffany: "I'm not fucking for a roof. I fuck people to heal them. Okay? I'm a healer. That's why I fuck, not for no roof over my head. I got a car. I got a roof."

Kevin: "Tiffany, you crazy as fuck. You should not be sleeping in your car. Here is $300, get yourself a hotel room for the week."

That was so nice of him, and I should have been more appreciative, but I had to point something out:

Tiffany: "What? I cannot get no hotel room nowhere for no week for three hundred bucks?"

He told me to write out a list of the goals I wanted to accomplish, like what I want out of life. I wrote the first thing on my list, "I want my own apartment."

The next day, I got a phone call from one of our mutual friends:

Friend: "Girl, there's an apartment for you. You should check it out. Kevin talked to some people, you should go check it out."

I went to check it out, and like—it was wack. The neighborhood was terrible. There were crackheads everywhere. It straight looked like the *Walking Dead* set or something. I pulled up to the apartment building. There were bars everywhere.

But I had this weird feeling—this place is secure. It's safe.

I ended up taking the apartment, and I fixed it up, and I still have it. The neighborhood is actually really nice now.

All thanks to my comedy guardian angel, Kevin Hart.

Tiffany's True
Hollywood Stories

Scientology

I think everyone who lives in LA has a Scientology story. Mine is pretty short. A lot of people think it's funny, but I didn't at the time. I still kind of don't.

I don't remember how I found Scientology. They offered me a place to stay for free, and this was during the period I was living out of my car. They said they would give me $50 a month to live there, and they would help me become a superstar.

That was cool and all, but I was really only interested in them because they told me they could take the hurt out of memories. I got some hurtful memories, that's for sure.

They were trying to get me to go do that thing they do, where you talk about your bad memories as you hold these metal handles, and they give you little electrical charges. You talk about what's making you so mad. I kept talking about my shit, and it was still reading high. They said, "Do it again, tell it again, tell it again." I must have told it fifteen times, twenty times, the thing was still reading off the charts. They told me to try again the next day.

Then they took me to the dorm. It was nothing but little white girls. I think the youngest one was seventeen and the oldest one was thirty. I was twenty-three or something. It was just me and them.

They took me to where I was going to sleep. It was bunk beds.

Tiffany: "Uh-uh. I can't live here, I cannot do that. You need to find me another place to sleep."

Scientologist: "No, Tiffany, this is where you sleep. It's very safe, and—"

Tiffany: "I don't fuck with bunk beds. Bad shit happens in bunk beds. I do not do that."

Scientologist: "Well, this is all we have, after all—"

Tiffany: "HELL NO! I'm gonna be trapped, y'all gonna let motherfuckers trap me. For what? $50 a month? That's how you're going to get me to sleep in a bunk? I don't think so, motherfucker. I AM OUT!"

I'm not a prima donna. Remember when I was in the orphanage—in state custody—we had bunk beds. And that was where the beatings happened.

Those older bitches used to beat my ass in the bunk bed. If

somebody is beating you up, and you get in that corner—you can't get up out of there. If you're in that bottom bunk and they're beating your ass, and there's walls on both sides, you cannot get out. There's no way out, you're trapped. You just get beat.

I know it's not rational, but those bunk beds just triggered it for me. I was going to be trapped in there. These weirdos started talking about Scientology to me.

Scientologist: "If you leave Scientology, you're breaking your bond, you're breaking—"

I went straight hood on them. I was screaming up and down the hallway.

Tiffany: "YOU MOTHERFUCKERS CAN'T PUT ME IN A BUNK BED TO GET MY ASS WHIPPED FOR $50 A MONTH!! THIS IS WHY THERE AIN'T NO BLACK PEOPLE IN THIS MOTHERFUCKER!!!"

Scientologist: "Tiffany, please, we're going to have to, you're going to have to go to the infirmary."

Tiffany: "Y'all said you was going to take the hurt from the memories. I'm still fucking hurt. SO FUCK YOU AND FUCK BUNK BEDS!!"

I know other people had problems leaving Scientology, but they let me the fuck out pretty quick.

Will & Jada

I was shooting the movie *Girls Trip* in New Orleans, and Jada Pinkett Smith was in it with me. We got to become pretty good friends on the set. One weekend, Will Smith was coming into town, and Jada invited me to dinner with her and Will.

I got all dolled up in my best cheap dress to go to dinner with them at this restaurant called La Petite Grocery. That place really lived up to its name. Despite being very expensive, it had very small portions of food. I ordered the short rib and it's just, like, one rib. Seriously, there's just a little morsel. There's one bite.

Tiffany: "Where's the rest of the meat?"

Jada: "You can order as many as you want, Tiffany. It's okay."

Tiffany: "Is this how y'all rich people stay thin, y'all just eat like, a bite of food and that's it? $30 for one bite? That's insane."

They also had crazy-expensive wine. I ain't into that. I asked the wine guy:

Tiffany: "Do y'all have Barefoot Moscato?"

They did have it, and they were cool about bringing it to me. Not snobby or anything.

If you don't know, Barefoot is that wine they sell in the grocery store real cheap. You can laugh at me. God knows Jada and Will were laughing at me.

Jada: "Oh man, Tiffany, it's you. It's you, Tiffany, it's you."

Tiffany: "What's so funny? You ever had Barefoot? It's good!"

Jada: "Yes, I've had it. I love hanging out with you, because you remind me of back when I was young, and living in Baltimore, just getting started. You just remind me of the good old days."

I thought, *Damn, your good old days must have sucked.*

She asked me what I was doing the next day, because we had the day off from shooting.

Tiffany: "Oh, I got me a Groupon, so I'm going on the swamp tour."

Jada: "Who you going with?"

Tiffany: "By myself."

Jada: "You going all by yourself?"

Tiffany: "Yeah, I don't have no friends out here in Louisiana, I'm going by myself."

Jada: "Well, maybe Will and I will go with you."

Tiffany: "Yeah right, y'all not gonna go with me."

Jada: "No, we'll probably go with you. We'll call you tomorrow and we'll see."

There was *no chance* Jada and Will were coming with me on a swamp tour. I just ignored that shit, and we had a great time at dinner.

The swamp tour was at about 2 p.m., so right after breakfast, I got out my weed that I had brought in from LA. Now, don't get all crazy—I have a prescription for this weed. I got real bad back pain, and my doctor agrees, and I have a prescription, so be cool.

I smoked a little, right? It was like twelve o'clock. I was thinking to myself, *Oh man, this swamp tour's gonna be so cool, I'mma smoke this weed and the alligators gonna be talking to me, the birds gonna be singing, the raccoons gonna be waving at me and stuff, it's gonna be like I'm in a Disney movie, it's gonna be great.*

And then about one o'clock, Jada called me. I was high as a kite.

Jada: "Hey Tiff, you still going on that swamp tour?"

Tiffany: "Yeah, of course I'm going."

Jada: "Well, Will and I are gonna go with you."

I paused for a second in disbelief.

Tiffany: "Wait, you're for real? Y'all really gonna go with me?"

Jada: "Yes."

Tiffany: "Okay cool. Don't even trip, y'all Groupon is on me, I got y'all. Since y'all paid for dinner last night, I'mma take care of you guys."

Now it was Jada's turn to pause.

Jada: "What?"

She told me to come to their hotel and we would ride together.

Tiffany: "Don't worry, I got it. I'll be over to your hotel in an hour."

OH SHIT!

So I started eating all this bread and drinking water, doing jumping jacks and freaking out. I gotta sober up and be cool.

An hour later, I pulled up to their hotel in my little $20-a-day rental car that I got. I started to hand my keys to the valet, 'cause I was thinking I'm gonna ride with Will and Jada and their security in the SUV, and it's gonna be all cool and stuff.

Nope.

Will Smith came running out the hotel like he's in *Bad Boys 7* and he jumped in the back seat of my car.

Will: "Whoa, it's been years since I've been in a regular car."

Then Jada runs in behind him.

Jada: "Oh my God, these windows aren't tinted, I don't feel safe."

Tiffany: "Really, Jada? You from Baltimore, bitch. Like for real?"

Jada: "Oh my goodness, fine let's go, right?"

Will: "Yeah, let's go, we don't want to be late."

So I started driving. The whole time, I was thinking I was lean-ing back in the seat driving all cool. But the next day, Jada told me I was up on the steering wheel. Of course I was up on the steering wheel, because all I could think was, *You don't want to be the chick on TMZ that killed the Fresh Prince of Bel-Air. Be careful, Tiffany. Drive carefully.*

I was trying to play music for them. I was playing the radio, and Chris Brown came on, and it was a new Chris Brown song. And it was so funny, because Will was bobbing his head, and every time I was looking in my rearview mirror, it was like, Will Smith was in my rearview mirror, smiling and bobbing his head.

I was thinking to myself: *This is fucking crazy. How could this be my life?*

Jada: "Who is this playing on the radio?"

Tiffany: "Oh, that's Chris Brown, you don't know who Chris Brown is?"

Jada: "I don't listen to his music, all I listen to is Shaolin monks."

I was like, *What? Is that what rich people listen to—monks? What the hell is she talking about?*

We pulled up to the swamp tour, and it was a lot of people out there waiting. Pretty much all of them white people, too.

Jada: "Tiffany, why are all these people here?"

Tiffany: "They probably all got Groupons."

Jada: "Tiffany, what is a Groupon?"

Tiffany: "What do you think it is?"

Jada: "I think it means you got your own boat that you could take a group of people on."

Tiffany: "No, Jada. It's a discounted coupon that you can do activities with. Why would you think that I had my own boat, Jada?"

Jada: "Will, you gotta go back to the hotel. Call security right now to come and get you to take you back to the hotel, because this gonna be a problem. With all these people and stuff, you need to go home, because it's gonna be pandemonium. But I'mma stay, 'cause they not gonna recognize me."

Will: "Oh, no fair. How you gonna invite me on the swamp tour and not let me go on the swamp tour? I want to go on the swamp tour."

Tiffany: "Yeah Will, tell your wife. Y'all gonna be safe, y'all with me, Tiffany Haddish. Ain't nothing gonna happen to y'all. I got my backpack, ain't nobody finna mess with us, we're gonna see what's on this swamp."

Jada: "You got a backpack?"

See, I was trying to make it seem like I had a weapon in my backpack, like I had it cracking. I was patting on the backpack like,

"We good, y'all. Like, ain't nobody finna mess with us, I'm from South Central LA, we finna have a good time, I promise you that."

Like I said, I was high. It made no sense.

Will: "Man, let's just go. Let's just do it. I came all the way out here, I want to get on the swamp tour."

Jada: "I don't know, I don't think it's gonna be okay, I don't know."

Tiffany: "Nobody's gonna bother us. I promise you ain't nobody gonna bother us."

I went in and got the tickets myself, and we were all set for one of the boats. I got Jada and Will out of the car, and we went to the boat, and nobody was saying nothing. This was 2016, everyone was on their phones, right?

Then this redneck dude with missing teeth yelled out, "Oh shoot, that's Will Smith, right there."

And everybody on the boat noticed, right as we stepped on the boat. They started clapping, everybody started hollering and cheering. I stepped on first, and I was like:

Tiffany: "Thank you, thank you everyone, thank you so much."

And people literally yelled out, "No, not you. Move out of the way!! Will, Jada! Oh my gosh!"

And I was like, *That's messed up. I'm the one who brought them!*

Redneck: "Hey Will, what part of Philadelphia you from?"

Will: "West Philadelphia."

Redneck: "Born and raised, right? Did you spend most of your days on the playground?"

Will: "Yeah. Yeah, man."

Redneck: "Can I get a picture?"

Then a girl jumped up and she asked if she can get a picture, and somebody else asked if they can get a picture, and then Will stood up:

Will: "Look, ladies and gentlemen, this is the Cajun swamp tour, not the Will Smith tour. So let's just enjoy ourselves and see what we can see, and once we're done on this tour, then maybe Jada and I will take pictures with you. Is that okay with everybody? Is that all right with everybody?"

Everyone cheered for him again. I was all mad and jealous, because he didn't even say anything funny, and they're cheering and clapping and laughing. *This is what fame and money does. I need to get some damn money.*

But it worked. We were just enjoying the swamp tour, and we were learning about nutria, which is the largest rodent. We learned about the different birds in the swamp. It was really beautiful. We saw like six alligators, and we got to feed marshmallows to the raccoons and alligators, it was really cool.

Will kept asking the tour guide a bunch of questions and stuff, and everybody was loving that, because Will Smith was talking.

Near the end of the tour, Will was just sitting there with his legs crossed, like how rich guys cross their legs, the ankle on the knee so their balls can drop, and he was just sitting there chilling.

Will: "Man, Tiffany, this is beautiful."

Tiffany: "I know, right?"

Will: "I'm gonna have to get me one of these."

Tiffany: "What, one of these boats?"

Will: "No, a swamp."

Tiffany: "What?!"

I was thinking to myself, *This nigga 'bout to buy an ecosystem?* I couldn't just let him top me, though.

Tiffany: "You know what, I'm gonna buy me something, too."

Will: "What?"

Tiffany: "I'm gonna buy me an iceberg, and I'm gonna melt it into yo swamp. Fuck up all yo complex ecosystem."

Will: "Hahahahahahaha. You're crazy, Tiffany."

Tiffany: "I might be. I might be crazy. Or maybe I'm just high as fuck."

Getting a Hollywood Assistant

Another thing Jada and Will talked to me about was getting an assistant. They insisted that I hire one.

They explained that having an assistant—giving somebody else the responsibility of the smaller things, the day-to-day things that you would normally do—helps you to be more focused on your art and your talent:

Jada: "Tiffany, you shouldn't have to be running the dogs to the groomer's or taking clothes to the dry cleaner's. That's an assistant's job. They should be helping you with that."

Tiffany: "Really?"

Jada: "Yes! You need peace and quiet for your art. Your assistant should be screening calls so you don't have to be talking to everybody, because you need your peace. It's very important to have your peace."

Tiffany: "I like peace and quiet."

Jada: "If you have an assistant, then they can take a lot of the worry and the stress off you. Because the more successful you get, the heavier the workload gets, and the more normal things that you would do, you can't do anymore, because you got other things to deal with. So give that responsibility to someone else."

So I hired a dude to be my assistant.

My lawyer wrote up the NDA, got it signed. And this guy worked for me for like a week. He was cool, very happy, and nice.

I fired him right away.

I just didn't feel comfortable with it. I don't know why. I feel like it's me giving up my power, and I can't give up my power.

I worked so hard to be independent and to have things for myself, and take care of myself. It's hard for me to let somebody else take care of me. Plus, I've been taking care of myself for so long.

He didn't do anything wrong. It's just me. I got trust issues.

One of my friends asked me why I felt this way. I think about it all the time. Part of it is my childhood and what I've been through. I could never really rely on anybody, I always had to do things myself. It's just hard changing those thought patterns, you know?

And also, I have trust issues with people being in my personal stuff. For example, I shop a lot online, I don't want nobody telling me, "Jeez, you're buying a lot of stuff from Amazon and Tophatter, why you got so many Groupons? Like, you're doing a lot of Groupon stuff, why are you doing all this stuff?"

For example, I bought two cases of wine off of Groupon, because they had unicorns on the bottle. I buy sex toys on Amazon. I buy all kinds of things that people think are stupid, and I AM TIRED OF EXPLAINING MYSELF!

I guess I should explain that, too. This was not my first attempt at hiring an assistant. I got baggage here, as well.

Two years ago, my best friend was my assistant. She did part-time work for me, assistant-type stuff. She was always in my business, criticizing me.

Friend: "Oh my God, Tiffany, why did you buy this?"

Tiffany: "Shut up. I'm gonna buy this stuff, I'll buy whatever I want to buy."

Friend: "But you're like, wasting money on gadgets that barely work."

Can you imagine having that conversation with someone? I don't want nobody telling me anything about how I spend my money.

I had to let her go. She was getting to be like my mama.

It all started when I shot this Tyler Perry series in Georgia. I needed help with getting a place to stay, learning my lines, and just getting settled in Georgia. One day, I had been talking to her on the phone, and I was like:

Tiffany: "Yeah, I gotta get somebody to help me find a spot out there."

Friend: "I'll help you. Shoot, I'm not working right now. You should let me work for you."

Tiffany: "Cool. But I can only afford like $400 a month."

Friend: "That's what's up. I'm just gonna be excited to be out there."

She helped me find this three-bedroom house that was only like $400 a month, so that was dope. And then she did everything for me, got the furniture for me, and she would do the grocery shopping. I had brought my dogs with me, so she would walk the dogs. And when I would get home from work, she would run the lines with me.

And she helped me with my emails. At the time I had like 8,000 emails that I hadn't even checked yet, so she checked all of them.

Yeah, I know. 8,000 unread emails. And a lot of them were important.

Friend: "Tiffany, you've got to check your emails more often. You know you probably missed twenty or thirty thousand dollars in comedy shows alone?"

Tiffany: "Wait—what?"

Friend: "So many people emailing you about doing comedy shows. Oh my God, Tiffany, you missed so much money not checking these emails."

A lot of them were recent, and I ended up making an additional four or five thousand dollars off a few of the emails.

When we were in Georgia, it was fun. When we got back to LA, I told her:

Tiffany: "I'm not working like that no more, and I don't really need an assistant."

Friend: "I'll just work anyways, I'll do it anyways. You don't need to pay me."

That did not work out. Basically, the next few months was just her questioning what I did and then telling me what to do.

Friend: "You need to go to bed."

Tiffany: "You ain't my mama!"

Friend: "Go to bed, Tiffany, you need to go to bed. You gotta go to work tomorrow."

Or when I was seeing this basketball player at the time, and she'd be like:

Friend: "You need to make him commit, he needs to make a commitment to you."

Tiffany: "He ain't your boyfriend, is he? I'm just enjoying him, leave me alone. I'm going to his game tonight."

Friend: "You don't have time for games, you're busy. You need to call your agent, you need to call your manager, you got a telephone interview at six, you got a set tomorrow . . ."

Just like, ALWAYS telling me what I needed to do.

Which was what I was paying her to do. I mean, she was really good at it.

I just had issues with that.

So yeah, I had to fire her. We are still friends, but we don't talk about money or my career anymore. It's not awkward though. At least not for me.

I know that I do need somebody reminding me what to do. I procrastinate on everything. Like right now. I should've went to the grocery store yesterday to get groceries, because I'm gonna cook for my brothers and sisters tomorrow, but I'm like, "Eh, the grocery store is twenty-four hours, I'll go later, I'll do it later."

Then when I get the groceries, it'll be two o'clock in the morning, and I'll get home, and I know I need to marinate this and do that and I'm just like, "Ah, I'll do it in the morning." Then I'll wake up in the morning and be like, "Ah, I'm still sleepy, I'll do it in a couple hours."

Then everybody'll be here, and then I'll be doing it. Everybody'll be waiting for the food and looking at me like, "Dang Tiff, you knew we was coming, didn't you?"

Okay, so yeah, I got problems.

But I don't want to be pestered about them!

How to Handle Backstabbing Bitches

My life is pretty good now, but sometimes I run into some motherfuckers and shit goes off. I'll tell you about this one time, very recently, I was at a wedding.

My boyfriend (at the time) and I were the only black couple there. We looked good. It was all white people and us. Very fancy wedding, lots of rich people, etc.

I went in the bathroom and was sitting in the stall peeing. Then, two ladies came in. They must have thought they were alone, because they started talking loud:

Old Lady 1: "You see that big, black butt that she got? Oh yeah, she could not fuck him right."

Old Lady 2: "We'll get her ass out of here, some way. We're going to fuck him. We're going to . . ."

And for ten minutes I heard them say terrible racist shit about me, and talk about getting my boyfriend to leave with them.

I just sat there, quiet. I was listening, getting madder and madder. I was two glasses of wine in already, so I was ready to fight these ladies. I sent a text message to Hollywood Friends 1 and 2 like:

"These old bitches at this wedding being racist as hell. I'm about to kick they asses. I'm sorry if I don't see you all for a while because I'm about to be in jail."

Hollywood Friend 1 called me immediately. Now mind you, I'm still sitting in the stall:

Hollywood Friend 1: "Tiffany, just leave. Just get an Uber right now and just walk out the door."

Tiffany: "I can't do it, I got to fight these bitches."

Hollywood Friend 1: "I'm not getting off the phone with you until you walk out the door. Just leave. Leave. Leave."

I opened the stall door, still on the phone with Hollywood Friend 1, and these two bitches gave me a look of shock and horror. They had no idea I was there.

Tiffany: "Okay, I will leave these fat-ass, Paula Deen–looking bitches to themselves, and get the hell out of this wedding."

I thought those women were going to straight die, right there in the bathroom.

I walked out, got my man, and we left. I was still steaming

when we got back to the hotel. We had some good sex that night, I tell you what. He thought it was funny that they wanted to fuck him.

Boyfriend: "You should have let them try. I would have put them on blast so bad."

The next day, Hollywood Friend 2 saw my text and called me. She stayed on the phone with me for two hours telling me about how racism works in Hollywood:

Hollywood Friend 2: "Honey child, let me explain. First off, what a blessing that you were able to hear them do it out loud, in your face. That's a blessing. I have been through so many experiences where they did it behind my back, or they just shut me down. That's what they do. They close you out. Be grateful that you got to hear it live and see it."

Tiffany: "How is that good?"

Hollywood Friend 2: "Because now you know those two are the enemy. Now you are aware. It's the ones that are sweet to your face and plotting behind your back that you have to worry about."

Tiffany: "Oh yeah. I hadn't thought about it that way."

Hollywood Friend 2: "The thing that's so bad about it is they do it to each other, too. Even worse. Them white women attack each other, and they go for each other's heads. Just imagine how they did you, imagine that times ten on each other. Their racism, is not even like racism. It's like sexism.

You're fucking a richer guy or a hotter guy, so now I'm going to destroy you."

Tiffany: "Yeah, I can see that."

Hollywood Friend 2: "Now imagine if you're a black woman and you're fucking a richer guy that they want to fuck. Now they're going to try to destroy you, because you're getting the dick they want and you're getting the money funneled down to you. See, boil it all down, Tiffany, it comes down to money and status. It ain't even about race."

Tiffany: "It's crazy, but yeah, I can see that. Oh my God. This sounds like Illuminati shit. But you're right. You trippin' me out. I feel like I'm watching a YouTube video."

Hollywood Friend 2: "At the end of the day, Tiffany, you just have to be gracious. You have to smile and when they say something you don't like, you figure out how to *Dallas* they ass."

Tiffany: "*Dallas*?"

Hollywood Friend 2: "*Knots Landing* they motherfucking ass. You got to get like a soap opera. You got to get down and dirty . . . but do it classy. Get down and dirty, but do it classy. Let these bitches know you not afraid to fuck them up."

Tiffany: "What do you mean? Should I fight?"

Hollywood Friend 2: "No, not with your hands! That's ghetto. With your words, with your actions, with your thoughts, with your success. You kill them with your success, Tiffany. You kill them with your success. Then they'll have to kiss your motherfucking feet."

Tiffany: "Yeah, I like the sound of that."

Hollywood Friend 2: "You do it right, and you're going to have these bitches walking behind you trying to clean your shit up, just like Oprah. You see what Oprah did? Them bitches will lick her ass. You know why? Because she killing them with her success. They've been racist towards her. They've been mean to her. They called her 'fat, black Harpo,' all that. Yeah, but who's on top? She says I like watermelon martinis, and boom—everybody drinking watermelon martinis now, Tiffany. Because Oprah said she liked them."

Tiffany: "Watermelon martinis is pretty good though."

Hollywood Friend 2: "Just stay focused, stay successful, and you shut these bitches down cleverly. Be smart and watch these soap operas, and stay classy, and you'll get there."

So now I watch soap operas for ideas on how to handle backstabbing bitches.

Hollywood Accounting

Me and my accountant get into it all the time.

Accountant: "What are you buying from PayPal, you're buying a lot of things from PayPal but it doesn't say exactly what it is."

Tiffany: "It's none of your business."

Accountant: "Tiffany, I cannot legally write it off your taxes unless you tell me what it is!"

So I told him. I had bought this book . . . I'm so fucking embarrassed about this, but I have to share it. Maybe it'll help me get past it. This book is basically how to get a man and how to get your ex back, or how to get a man to be into you, right? It's by this guy who's like a relationship advisor guy, and to be a member of his thing is like $39.99 a month, and you get a book and text messages and stuff.

Accountant: "What is this $39.99 a month, what's this for?"

Tiffany: "For my education, it's an educational program."

Accountant: "For what?"

Tiffany: "For guys, to know men better. It helps me in my comedy."

Accountant: "I can't write that off."

Tiffany: "Yeah-huh! It's relationship stuff, and I talk about relationship stuff in my comedy."

I fuss with him about all kinds of things.

Accountant: "You can't use business credit cards to buy weed, Tiffany, that's not cool. That's health stuff."

Tiffany: "It's my medicine. I have a prescription from a doctor. So I can ease my back pain and get onstage and perform. So you have to write that off, too."

I buy too much weird stuff that pisses him off. I bought a $300 microscope, because I'm into science.

Accountant: "You can't write off a microscope! It does not affect your business. How does that help you with acting or comedy?"

Tiffany: "Well, it helps me with comedy, because I talk about bacteria and stuff onstage, and I have to research the bacteria, so I'm not giving off false information."

He didn't believe me, so he brought his buddy to the comedy show, to my special, and he's like:

Accountant: "Yep, this is who I was telling you about, with the microscope and the seducing men books."

I got all angry—don't tell everybody that!
Of course, I'm writing about it here, which is worse. But damn, that's my decision to spread my business, not his!

Queen Latifah's House Party

Queen Latifah had a party at her house and invited me. I asked her if I could bring a couple of my comedian friends, Hannibal Buress and Lil' Rel.

Queen Latifah: "Do they got something to lose?"

Tiffany: "What?"

Queen Latifah: "You never invite nobody to your house, unless they got something to lose."

Tiffany: "Well, they're pretty popular entertainers, so I think they got something to lose."

Queen Latifah: "Yeah, okay, well they welcome to come. Long as they got something to lose."

So we all went to her house, and it was Fourth of July. She's having a party, and we were drinking and having a good time. All kinds of famous people were there. I was in the pool, standing there, drinking and talking to Larenz Tate and his brothers.

I heard a voice that I recognized. I turned and looked, then turned back to the guys and said:

Tiffany: "You guys, is that Mary J. Blige, or am I tripping?"

Larenz: "No, that's Mary J. Blige."

I started backstroking towards her, all smooth right? And I was like:

Tiffany: "Hey girl, how you doing?"

And I just started talking to her, but I was so drunk.

Tiffany: "Me and my friends, we love your music, we used to bump it all the time, we still be bumping it."

And I started singing some of her songs to her, and she was laughing.

Mary: "What do you do?"

I got out the water, but I had been drinking so much that I was bloated, so my swimming suit was crawling up in my butt, it was just looking bad. So I'm trying to dig my swimming suit out my ass, and Mary J. Blige was looking at me crazy.

Tiffany: "I know you looking at me crazy, but look, I just signed a modeling contract."

Mary: "You did?"

Tiffany: "Yep, with Big Lots. I'm a swimsuit model for them. Regular body edition, girl."

And she just fell out laughing.

Mary: "You crazy, girl!"

So Mary offered me a drink, or maybe three, or six, and I don't remember too much after that. Music had come on, I started dancing and stuff. I was just having a good time, but I know eventually that Queen Latifah came over and got me and was like:

Queen Latifah: "Tiffany, it's time to go in the house, you tripping."

Tiffany: "Am I being bad?"

Queen Latifah: "Girl, yo ass is crazy. You need to go in the house."

So she took me in the house, and I just fell asleep immediately.

That's right, I FELL ASLEEP. I did not PASS OUT. I was just tired, and so I went to SLEEP.

Lil' Rel and Hannibal put sunglasses on me. When I was ASLEEP. They would take turns closing my mouth 'cause my ass was light snoring every time my mouth opened, and it was bothering everyone who was playing games like Taboo and Spades.

The next day at the movie set, Queen Latifah was clowning me.

Queen Latifah: "Tiffany, you was so funny. You was just dancing all crazy. I haven't seen Mary J. Blige laugh like that in years."

Tiffany: "For real?"

Queen Latifah: "You was the only person that was talking to her, besides me and her sister, and Mary said she really enjoyed you."

Tiffany: "Really?"

Jada: "Yeah girl, it was fun."

Tiffany: "Jada, you was at the party, too?"

They thought that shit was real funny, that I didn't even know Jada was at the party. I guess I SLEPT a lot.

A few weeks later, Mary J. Blige's security texted me up:

Security: "Hey, you need to hang out with Mary more, she going through her divorce and stuff, and she said that you her favorite comedian, that you are so funny, she had such a good time with you. You need to come hang out with us."

If my sixteen-year-old self had seen that text, I would have died. Right there on the curb, dead.

But my thirty-five-year-old self had a TV show to film! I had just got back on *The Carmichael Show*, so I couldn't really hang out, I just didn't have the time.

So yeah: Mary J. Blige wanted me to come hang out, and I was like, "I would love to, but I don't have the time."

Sorry, Mary! But for real, hit me up again when you in LA, girl. I got my Big Lots modeling money, we'll do it right!

Dave Chappelle

I did a show one time (not in LA, in Ohio), and Dave Chappelle showed up to the show. When he came off stage, he was like:

Dave: "Tiffany, you're a genius."

DAVE CHAPPELLE THINKS I'M A GENIUS!

I wasn't about to let this moment pass by, though. I immediately hit him up.

Tiffany: "Thank you, thank you. I'm trying to work on doing my own show, I'd love for you to be on my show."

Dave: "What show you trying to do?"

Tiffany: "It's called Judge Ratchet, and I'm the judge, and I'm taking cases that you can't take to real court."

Dave: "Like what?"

Tiffany: "Like, if somebody a dope dealer, and they lose their dope, 'cause somebody get arrested with it or whatever, and then they sue them, 'cause they want their money. They want the dope back, or they want the money back. Baby mamas tripping, just really stupid stuff, stuff you can't take to real court."

Dave: "Ah, that's genius, I'mma do it."

Tiffany: "Cool, perfect, when you gonna be in town?"

Dave: "No time soon!"

I was like, okay. At least he was nice about blowing me off.

But now every time I run into him or I see him, he's like, "You are so good, you're a genius." He's always telling me I'm a genius, so that makes me feel good. But he didn't ever show up.

Dave is supposed to be all anti-Hollywood, but ain't that about the most Hollywood thing ever—a star promising shit that they don't deliver on? (I'm kidding, I love you Dave!)

She Ready

How I Knew I Made It

I knew I made it in Hollywood when I went on *The Arsenio Hall Show*.

That's kind of a weird specific marker to be my "when I made it" story, so let me explain.

I remember being a kid watching Arsenio. He was my idol. I remember wishing he was like my dad or my big brother or something like that. I would watch every single show, every minute of it.

I got in so much trouble for that, too. Because it came on at eleven at night, I would sneak in the closet and watch him on my little black-and-white TV. My mom used to beat me out the closet all the time over that.

Being a guest on his show was a dream for so long. When he went off the air in 1994, I thought I missed my shot.

Then, in 2013, he came back on the air. I got so excited. This could be my chance to get on there, and now that I'm a working comedian, I got a real shot, right?

Of course, I had to update my fantasy, too. Now that I'm older, maybe instead of him being my daddy, he could be my baby daddy.

I had a friend who got booked on the show, and he invited me to go with him. I met the talent booker, and she said maybe they could use me for a few sketches. I told her she could use me to clean toilets, if it got me on the show.

They used me to shoot this sketch called "I Married a Black Woman." I gave 110 percent in that performance. The producers liked it, and they decided to have me come back again, and then for a third time. By the third one, I had been pitching them relentlessly on doing my stand-up, and they finally agreed to book me.

Tiffany: "Will I finally get to meet Arsenio?"

Producer: "Yeah, you'll meet him, of course. On the show."

Tiffany: "When I meet Arsenio, I'm telling y'all right now, I'm going to jump on him and I'm going to kiss him all over his face, and I'm going to tell him that he's my favorite and that I want to have all his babies."

Producer: "He already has kids. He has a son."

Tiffany: "Yeah, but he don't have a full black baby, and I could give that to him."

Producer: "Uh . . . okay."

Tiffany: "And I want to tell him I used to get whippings for him. I used to get in trouble for him. I got beat out the closet for him. I want him to know this!!"

Producer: "Okay, okay, Tiffany, you'll meet him afterwards, no problem."

I was a little crazy, I know, but this was my idol growing up.

So the day came, and I was off stage about to go on, and I heard him talking about me. He said something like:

Arsenio: "This next comedian coming to the stage, guys, not only is she beautiful, and funny, but she's smart."

I thought I was going to die right there. I swear, I was crying. There was tears coming out of my eyes. I was crying with joy.

Producer: "You okay?"

Tiffany: "ARSENIO SAID I WAS SMART AND BEAUTI-FUL! DID YOU NOT HEAR THAT!! OH LORD THANK YOU LORD!"

Producer: "Pull yourself together, girl! You about to go out there!"

Tiffany: "Oh my God, oh my God, oh my God."

I mean, that was like the biggest thing in the whole wide world.

I remember watching the video of me coming out onstage, and it looks like I was so confident and so self-assured. But inside, I was crying baby tears of joy, because Arsenio said I was smart. I did the set, and it was a great performance, but honestly, I don't think I was mentally present for any of it. I was just so . . . I don't know. Honestly, I was wet thinking about what he said.

When I was done, the whole crowd was cheering and clapping, and Arsenio came over to me. In my mind, I was about to jump on him and kiss him all over his face. But he scooped me up and picked me up and held me like a baby! So I guess the producer obviously told him I was going to jump on him.

He picked me up like a baby, and I was like, oh my God—I just started licking his face.

I couldn't help myself. I was so happy.

Straight up—his face tastes just like Ovaltine. I think that they use Ovaltine for his foundation because he's so chocolatey, I don't know. But it tasted amazing.

I ended up being on there seven times. I came back as a correspondent for him. I would go into the audience, and be all over the studio, doing different funny things. And people really loved it. But then the show got canceled shortly thereafter.

That was the moment that started it all and led to everything— even this book. That was where I met Tyler Perry. He saw my "I Married a Black Woman" sketch, and he had me come in and audition. Then he hired me for a show. That led to me getting *The Carmichael Show*. From there, I booked movies like *Keanu* and *Girls Trip*.

I know it came from me and my hard work, but still, Arsenio Hall gave me a platform to be able to be seen being me. And I'm so grateful to him for that. That was pretty huge.

Oh, and it gets better!

We went to dinner!

We went to a late dinner, and I thought this was it. I thought this was going to be my chance. I was single right then. He was single right then. I know he old enough to be my dad, but I don't care. I'll help him raise his son. I'll give him a full black baby. He was saying how he was a foodie, and hey, I like to eat food, too.

It was a really, really great dinner, and we laughed and had an amazing time. I thought I was going to get a kiss. I thought I was going to come up on something. But no. He just said, "Let's go out to eat again."

I was not aggressive with him, because I was trying not to be thirsty, like I was in high school and still am sometimes. It was real hard for me not to just blurt out: "What's up with that dick, Arsenio?"

I wanted to, but I didn't. I didn't. I just told him he had very nice hands and that I loved his fingers. That's all I said. I didn't get too thirsty on him, though. But I sure wanted to.

Mama

My mom is still alive. She is in a mental institution in Riverside.

One time she was arrested, they took her to this place in Norwalk. They were healing her. Whatever medicines they was giving her, whatever they was doing, it was like she was normal.

I would go see her, and she was my mama. She didn't say anything mean or try to hit me. She hugged me. She held me. We talked. I felt like I was six, seven years old again. Before the accident.

She asked me to get her out of there, so I did. Then she stopped taking that medication, and she went right back to beating my ass and being my crazy mom again.

She never hit any of my brothers and sisters or anything. She might cuss at them, but she didn't hurt them. I asked her about that just recently.

Tiffany: "Mom, why you always try to fight me, but you don't ever try to fight my siblings?"

Mama: "You look just like me, and I don't like that."

Tiffany: "So, you're beating yourself up?"

Mama: "I guess so. I don't like that you look like me, though. And you look like your ugly-ass daddy."

Tiffany: "Now you gotta stop saying that, Mama, 'cause he's not ugly. He's not ugly. I've seen him. He's not ugly."

Mama: "Mm-hm. Maybe not to you."

Tiffany: "Not to you either, you opened your legs to the man for three years."

Then she popped me in the mouth. Dammit, I'm thirty-seven years old, still getting popped in the fucking mouth.

My goal is to get enough money to buy a duplex. I want to put her in one of the units and hire a full-time nurse to take care of her. Then, I want to get her on whatever medications they gave her when she was in Norwalk, so she can be my mama again.

Honestly, that's all I really want from life.

How to Survive and Thrive in Hollywood

When I was hanging out with Jada in New Orleans shooting *Girls Trip*, I had a knockoff Michael Kors bag, and the lock fell off.

Jada: "You need real bags, you can't be running around here with fake bags, what kind of bag is that?"

Tiffany: "This is my Martin Luther King bag. The lock fell off, so it's free at last. Get it?"

Jada: "No, I don't get it. It's a fake. You have to get real designer stuff. You can't be having knockoff stuff."

Tiffany: "Well, that's the kind of money I got, knockoff money, so that's probably what kind of bag I should have, right?"

She shook her head and laughed at me. Later that week, she decided to go back to LA for the weekend, and invited me to go with her.

Tiffany: "That sounds fun, but how we gonna book a ticket this late? It'll be too expensive. And I bet first class is filled up."

Jada: "Book a ticket? Girl, we're taking a private jet to LA."

Tiffany: "Oh, I can't. I'm not getting on no private jet."

Jada: "Why?"

Tiffany: "Aaliyah. Never forget."

Jada: "What?"

Tiffany: "Aaliyah, never forget! La Bamba, too."

Jada: "What the fuck are you talking about?"

Tiffany: "Right when you are about to blow the fuck up, when you about to get hella super famous and have hella unlimited amounts of money, that's when you get killed. And it's always in a small plane. Unless there is ten white people on that flight, I cannot get on that flight."

Jada: "Something is wrong with your brain."

Tiffany: "Your husband said that to me, too."

When she was in LA, I posted a picture of myself on Instagram in a dress I thought was nice. Jada hit me up on text:

Jada: "Get a better dress."

She sent me all these links to these designer dresses, but they're like $500.

Tiffany: "Jada, I feel very fly in my $85 dress."

Jada: "Who made it, Tiffany?"

Tiffany: "Who cares? It look good."

Jada: "lol, you keep doing you, Tiffany ☺ I'll explain when I get back."

She came back from LA, and she gave me this nice bag, a Givenchy. It had this huge picture of a barking dog on the side. It was mean-looking.

Tiffany: "What's up with the dog?"

Jada: "Oh, I know you can't afford security, so this should keep the mopes off you."

Tiffany: "Thank you, Jada, that is so sweet."

She left the price tag on, it was like $1200. I was like, *Oh yeah! I struck gold.*

Tiffany: "Oh my God, I'm taking this right to the pawn-shop, and I'm gonna get my light bill paid for the rest of the year."

Jada: "You cannot do that, that's bad luck."

Tiffany: "What are you talking about?"

Jada: "You've got to use it for at least six months before you can give it away. Or sell it. That is how you have to deal with a gift."

Tiffany: "Oh, that's what rich people do?"

Jada: "Yes Tiffany . . . it's what we do."

Tiffany: "Seriously though, Jada, I can't be keeping this. This is too much."

Jada: "It's fine, it's a gift from me. And I didn't pay for it, the designers gave it to me."

Tiffany: "Oh you got it free? Is that how you so rich, you get all this expensive shit for free?"

She started laughing at me.

Tiffany: "But seriously, I can't have this. My philosophy is that if I can't keep the amount of money in there that it costs, I shouldn't have it. However much a bag costs, if the bag is a $300 bag, I should be able to keep $300 in it at all times, or it's too expensive."

Jada was laughing at me again.

Jada: "Well, Tiffany, why don't you just put $1200 in there?"

Tiffany: "I can't keep that much cash on me! This fake dog ain't gonna stop robbers!"

Jada: "Well it's a gift, and it's the type of nice designer bag you should have. You need to find a way to use it."

I thought about it, and came up with a great idea.

Tiffany: "Okay, I'll get a money order for $1200 in there that's made out to myself. That way, I can always have $1200 in my bag. For myself, and can't nobody steal it!"

More laughing from Jada. I don't know if she thinks my actual comedy is this funny.

She gave me three more Givenchys and a wallet (I was calling it

Gio-van-nucci for like, two weeks, 'cause I can barely read, but it's Givenchy). She left the price tags on everything.

Tiffany: "Why are you leaving the prices on if you got it free?"

Jada: "So you know the value of what you're carrying around. You got to carry yourself like you're valuable, and you need to have valuable things. When this movie comes out, you're going to be an A-list actress, you've got to think like an A-list person. This is what I was talking about in that text I sent you."

Tiffany: "What do you mean? I like my $85 dress."

Jada: "Tiffany, you want to wear designer clothes, because people are going to be seeing you, you're gonna be in the eye of the public and they're gonna be like, what are you wearing? If you say Chico or Ann Taylor, that's not going to work. You need to be wearing designers. It sets you apart from everybody else and puts you in a certain class level. If you want to be considered top-notch, you need to wear top-notch type things."

Tiffany: "But Jada, this stuff costs money. I appreciate your gifts, I really do, but I can't buy this myself. I have to be smart with my money, and save it. I gotta stack my chips, not spend 'em."

Jada: "You absolutely should be smart with your money! If it makes you feel safe to stack your chips, stack 'em. Most people in Hollywood don't do that, that's smart."

Tiffany: "I want to spend my money on things that I think will make me more money. That's why I'm investing in my book. And my comedy special. That's why I buy nice hair, it's going to make me more money if I look better, like that."

Jada: "That's great, Tiffany, you do that. That's what I'm talking about."

Tiffany: "OK, but what I still don't get is what does a $1200 bag have to do with that? If I buy shit like that, I'll be broke. I need my knockoffs, they keep me from living in my car again."

Jada: "Tiffany, your only two options are not either (1) spend all of your money to try and fit in, or (2) be cheap and look low-class. There are other options, girl!"

Tiffany: "Like what? I'm not about to steal that stuff!"

I couldn't think of any other options from what she said, besides stealing.

Jada: "I'll introduce you to some people, but really, all it boils down to is using your fame to get the stuff. Designers want famous, pretty women wearing their clothes. You put yourself on Instagram wearing a $500 dress, most places will give it to you for free, or very cheap."

Tiffany: "Free is an option? Because I understand free, and I like that shit a lot. Free does make sense."

I have thought about this a lot, and the more experience I get in Hollywood, the more I think Jada is right. I definitely have a very rough mentality, a broke person's mentality. I have a little bit of money now, but I just stack it away like a chipmunk. I don't know how much to spend, or where, or on what. It's cool to save, but I need to use my money in smart ways to help myself and my career.

Now that I've earned my way to a new level in life, I have to do new things. I can't be living that poor life anymore, I can't be thinking that way. Poor mindset can work when you're poor, but it doesn't work well when you have a little money (I emphasize a little—I'm *far* from rich).

I know this, but honestly, part of me still feels like I could end up homeless again at any point in time, and then all I'm going to have is a bag with a dog on it. And I don't want that. I'd rather have the money.

I want my money to make me money, but what Jada is teaching me is that how you look in Hollywood can often make you money. Opportunities in Hollywood will open up if you are sending the right signals about yourself. Fashion is part of how to send the right messages.

If I want to be the girl that belongs in Hollywood, I not only have to have talent, but I also have to signal to Hollywood that I belong.

By wearing cheap, low-class, knockoff stuff, I'm telling people that they can treat me low-class. That maybe I don't belong on that higher level.

I have to value myself properly. That's something I have had a hard time with in the past, but I'm getting better.

Jada: "Tiffany, I'm also going to need you to be wearing makeup when you're out or onstage. And can you at least glue on some lashes and put on some lips daily?"

Tiffany: "I don't feel like it. If it's an audition? Yeah. If it's an interview for something? Yeah. Otherwise, I feel like I should be able to walk around here naked-faced."

Jada gave me that look you give a child when they are mad that gravity exists.

Jada: "Tiffany, that *should* be how it works. And it would be great if it was true. But it's not how Hollywood works. You need to start wearing makeup. You're a pretty girl, you need to let yourself look that way."

Tiffany: "Okay, well when we get closer to the premiere of the movie, I'll start wearing makeup, I promise. And it'll be good makeup too, not the stuff I buy from the pharmacy."

She laughed at that, too.

Daddy

My father just died on May 13, 2017.

I'm looking at him right now, his cremated remains, as I write this. He's in a priority mail box, sitting on my dresser.

He didn't want me at the hospital or anything. When he visited me in LA, he went to the hospital. He told the doctors not to tell me anything that's going on with him. I know that he had congestive heart failure, but he wouldn't tell me anything else.

Tiffany: "Dad, well, if you don't let them tell me, what do you want me to do? What if you die?"

Dad: "I want you to cremate my body and take me back to Africa and put me next to my mother."

He told the hospital not to call me or contact me until he was dead. They called me just before he died, because they felt like that was wrong. I flew up there, paid for the mortuary, everything.

I called one of his cousins to tell him. He started telling me about all this property I got in Africa, and that I'm actually a princess in his old village. That my dad was like a king in the village, but he ran away because of the war. Then he was saying, there's back taxes that I need to pay and all this stuff. And if I come, I have to come with some type of security, because it's still a war going on in the village, where my grandmother's grave is. And I have to claim this land for the family, before the government finds out my father is dead, because they'll confiscate it from the family, and then we won't have nothing, and that's what they living off of.

I didn't know about any of this. This feels like it's a movie. Hopefully, not a tragedy.

I just know that I married a man who promised to find my daddy. I got ten years with my dad. I learned a lot, but I also feel like he punked out on me.

Now he wants me to go to Africa. I don't know. I am trying to find the funny in that. I still can't find nothing funny about it, but I'm trying.

She Ready Now

The movie *Girls Trip* came out in July 2017, did thirty million in the opening weekend, and my life totally changed.

This used to be my normal conversation with directors and producers:

Tiffany: "Hey, I would like to work with you one day."

Producer: "Ha, yeah, you're a good comedian."

Tiffany: "You best get on the Tiffany train while you can, because it's about to take off."

Then they all just blew me off.

Now those same directors and producers are blowing my phone up.

The day after the movie came out, I had a hundred text messages.

The next morning when I woke up, four hundred text messages.

That week, I got probably fifteen hundred different people texting me wanting to get together or work together or pitch me on something.

Now, mind you, fifty of the texts were from my ex-husband, trying to get me back. Three of them were from Titus, trying to have lunch and sit down with me at some point, and four other ex-boyfriends sending all kinds of stuff. But still, most were from real Hollywood people.

I gotta admit, that shit feels *real good*.

Honestly, part of me doesn't want to work with those people.

The people that I asked to give me a chance, the ones who said no, I kinda want to just ignore them. I mean, I'm not going to do that, it's not professional, but still—I kinda want to.

The funniest part is that Rumpelstiltskin is all over me now. Remember that dude, the one who said, "The only way you can go on tour with me is if you putting out"?

Rumpelstiltskin called me the week after the movie came out:

Rumpelstiltskin: "Hey Tiff, my mom said that you amazing and that I'm a fool for not having you on my shows and stuff. I should have been working with you a long time ago."

Tiffany: "Your mama right, she a smart woman. I told you that, too."

Rumpelstiltskin: "Yeah, so how would you feel about doing a tour with me, you, some other comedians. How do you feel about that?"

Tiffany: "I don't know. You headlining it?"

Rumpelstiltskin: "No, no, no, no, no. I'm going to host. You be the headliner. You the main attraction. You the big deal."

Tiffany: "I'm listening."

Rumpelstiltskin: "I talked to your people, they say you get a thousand dollars a minute."

Tiffany: "That's right. It used to be a dollar a minute. Now it's a thousand dollars a minute. That's right."

Rumpelstiltskin: "Oooo, that's a little steep. How about if we do thirty-four shows, and half of them will be in theaters and the other half will be in arenas. How would you feel about making eighteen-five a show?"

Tiffany: "Eighteen thousand five hundred dollars?"

Rumpelstiltskin: "Yeah."

Tiffany: "Mm, I don't know. That's half my normal fee."

Rumpelstiltskin: "Yeah, but all you got to do is show up!"

Tiffany: "I can't even say that I'm going to be able to show up at all. See, Kevin Hart just called me and asked me to do a movie with him. So, I'm gonna do the movie. 'Cause that's a A-list movie."

Rumpelstiltskin: "Well, maybe we can work around your movie schedule."

Tiffany: "Well, see, I already have my own shows booked. A bunch of them. I mean, you have to work around the dates I already have booked. You know how it is—I'm headlining my own shows. They're already sold out, most of 'em. So, I don't know what to tell you, man. I don't know what to tell you."

Rumpelstiltskin: "You can tell me yes."

Tiffany: "I think you really shouldn't even be talking to me. You need to be talking to my team."

Rumpelstiltskin: "But I'm talking to you first, because I want to make sure it's cool with you before I present it to your team."

Tiffany: "Well, you need to present it to my team. Then if they present it to me in a manner that it seems like it's financially feasible, then I will take that on."

Rumpelstiltskin: "Okay, okay, I will do that. Right away."

Tiffany: "Also, I need you to tell my people who's putting out on this tour. I'll need to know that."

Rumpelstiltskin: "What?"

Tiffany: "Who's putting out on this tour, 'cause I know it ain't me."

Rumpelstiltskin: "Tiffany, Tiffany, those was jokes. Those was jokes. You KNOW those was jokes."

Tiffany: "Yeah, maybe. Except, you never did let me come on tour with you. If it was a joke, you would have booked me, if it was a joke."

Rumpelstiltskin: "Don't be holding on to old shit. Let that shit go now. Just let that shit go. Let it go. That's the past. That's the past. We living in the now."

Tiffany: "Yeah, I don't know about that, Rumpelstiltskin, sound like somebody about to make a whole lotta money, and it ain't gonna be me. I don't know."

Rumpelstiltskin: "Girl, you must be about to start your period. I'm gonna call you back."

Two days later, he called back.

Rumpelstiltskin: "We put the offer in to your people, Tiffany. Now you just gotta tell them you want to do it."

Tiffany: "Yeah, okay. But it sound like to me, somebody is trying to eat off of my plate. I don't know if a thousand dollars a minute gonna get it anymore. I really don't know if that's gonna get it. You know?"

Rumpelstiltskin: "Well shit, if you do forty minutes, that's forty thousand dollars."

Tiffany: "I know, right? And if you sold out an arena, and you selling tickets for $50 to $150 a ticket, shit, that's going to be more than that. That's going to be a lot more. Well into the six figures. I mean, I'm going to need to make some money, too."

Rumpelstiltskin: "Who are you right now?"

Tiffany: "I'm Tiffany-Motherfucking-Haddish, who I always been! Rumpelstiltskin, I like you, I really do, but you not going to take advantage of me, Rumpelstiltskin. That's not going to happen."

Rumpelstiltskin: "Ah baby, you hilarious. You hilarious."

Tiffany: "Nah, but for real, go talk to my team, and I will discuss it with them, and they will get back to you later."

I just hung up the phone.

Oh BOY, that call felt good!!

I was so close to saying this to him: "Yeah, I'll do it, if you open up that booty hole. You gotta open up that booty hole for me, though."

I didn't say that, though. I sure wanted to, but I didn't. Rumpelstiltskin may not be a great person, but he's not a bad person. He's all right, he doesn't deserve that sort of treatment. And it's unprofessional, and I'm not going to be like that.

But seriously, that's the kind of stuff that's been going on. A lot of people that told me I couldn't make it, or tried to take advantage of me, now they are trying to figure out a different way to take advantage or be on my team in some kind of way.

But that's not going to happen. I'm a survivor, and all this struggle I went through—while it sucked at the time—is really helping me now. It has helped me get to where I am, and it will help me continue to improve and do better.

It didn't always feel like it at times, but I truly believe I am blessed.

We Not Done

Growing up, I just wanted to feel wanted.

I often think about having kids. Since I am single as fuck and getting older, I'm thinking I will adopt a kid. Maybe an eight-year-old or a nine-year-old, something like that.

I was in that spot. When you're like ten and a foster kid, nobody wants you around, because they think you're done. There's no way you're going to come out from that situation undamaged.

I remember when I was in school, the social worker was like, "Her comprehension is not good."

I comprehended very well. I knew what they was talking about. I was just quiet, because I didn't want to get popped. Because there was popping at the school back then, in the hood in South Central. Them teachers would slap the shit out your ass.

Before high school, I didn't talk much. When I did talk, I was on the playground. I would want to play with the boys, because if somebody picked on me while I was playing basketball, the other dudes would be like, "Man, leave her alone. She's with us." They would protect me.

That's what I wanted. Someone to protect me. Something to be part of.

Eventually, I realized the only thing I could really be a part of was drama or being the mascot or working the Bar Mitzvahs. That's the only way I could feel included.

What did they all have in common?

Entertainment. Performing. Being something that other people wanted me to be. Those were the only things I'd be included in.

Not to be Tiffany. To be outside of myself. Because myself wasn't necessarily . . . I felt like I wasn't good enough. Just being me wasn't good enough. Not for my parents, not for school, not for anything.

I got into the entertainment business so I could feel accepted. And loved. And safe.

When I go onstage to do comedy, it's about me. I feel accepted for who I am. I can go onstage with my hair fucked up, no makeup, ugly-ass clothes I've been wearing for three days, and people still appreciate me. They still laugh.

Being onstage is my safest place. It's the only place I've ever felt like nobody's going to jump up and beat me, and if somebody do beat me, there's so many people in here they're going to stop it.

And it's onstage where my voice is heard. I'm not being shut out. It's where I am accepted.

I just shot my special in a theater that seats four hundred people. They had to turn lots of people away. Those people came to see me. Whether it was to see me succeed or to see me fail, they still came for me.

It's a safe place, like I'm being loved and admired. I know it's not really that, but it's the closest I've ever really had, so far.

I didn't start out with the intention of writing about all this painful stuff. I just wanted to write a funny book.

I don't normally like getting all deep into painful shit. I like to skip across the ocean of emotion. I feel like that's better.

But once I started working on this book, I got into all this shit. If something comes up, I'm going to talk about it. I'm going to tell you about it, and if it hurts, that's too bad. I'm going to be like, "Yo, that shit hurt, but let me tell you though."

That's who I am.

I feel like, honestly, that's the only reason I'm still alive. Because I'm willing to talk about my stuff. Whether it's onstage, or with friends, or in this book.

I think that's why I came back to comedy, after being out of it for a while in my teens and early twenties. So I had a place to talk about my painful stuff, to share it, and to do it in a way that worked, and helped out other people, too.

My friend told me that people who haven't lived anything even close to a life like mine, even they think they are the fucked up ones, and that everyone else is normal:

> *Friend:* "Tiffany, *everyone* has some version of this in their life. Everyone has their own personal pain and their own demons, and no one will talk about it, and that's why they never get better. They're all afraid to talk about it."

I guess I'm not afraid to talk about it.

It just hurts a lot when I do.

I believe in God. And I believe I have a purpose in life. I believe we all do. I believe you do, too.

I believe my purpose is to bring joy to people, to make them laugh, and to share my story to help them. To show people that no matter what, they matter, and they can succeed. No matter how bad things go, no matter how dark your life is, there is a reason for it. You can find beauty in it, and you can get better. I know, because I've done it.

That's why my comedy so often comes from my pain. In my life, and I hope in yours, I want us to grow roses out of the poop.

Acknowledgments

TIFFANY HADDISH

I want to thank:

My Grandma.

My Mama.

My Aunties.

My Daddy for donating the sperm that made me.

All my brothers and sisters.

My best friends Selena, Shermona, Aiko, Shana, Richea.

My old agent, my current agents and managers, and Tucker Max.

Department of Children Services and the court system for taking care of me when no one else would.

I want to thank EVERYONE who ever said anything positive to me or taught me something. I heard it all, and it meant something.

All the dudes I ever slept with, I appreciate the experiences, but I ain't naming none of you!

I want to thank God most of all, because without God I wouldn't be able to do any of this.

TUCKER MAX

First, I have to thank Tiffany.

I've turned down every other celeb who asked me to cowrite their book, but I took on this book because I believed Tiffany would do something no one else would do.

She promised me she would lay it all out there . . . and she did.

This book is deep and so real in a way that very few other books are. She's created something special. I'm proud of her and proud to have worked on it.

The other group I have to thank is my team at Book in a Box. I cofounded a company that helps people write and publish their books, and though I am the name behind it, they do most of the work and deserve the props. Without them, this doesn't happen.

If you like this book, the credit goes to Tiffany, and to my team. Enjoy.